CW00644755

ACKNOWLDEGEMENTS

This book is dedicated to our parents Ed and Ellie. It was our pleasure caring for both of you. We would not be people we are today if it wasn't for your wonderful care of us when we were kids.

I personally would like to thank all of you children who have decided to care for your parents the way we have taken care of ours. It is the toughest job our family has ever had to do. It has brought me so much pain and so much joy, I can't begin to explain.

I also want to thank my husband, Jerry and our kids, Emily and Aaron who had to put up with turning our kitchen into a mass production factory. I know I have spent numerous hours away from you to be able to care for Mom and Dad. THANK YOU! I LOVE YOU!

Oh, and I can't forget my sisters, Anna and Joan, and my gal-pal Kelley, who put in the hours with me in the kitchen and with all the parental care. THANK YOU!!!

Tom and Mary you have provided much mental support for our family even though you couldn't physically be in Texas with Mom and Dad.

Roxie, thank you for your wonderful typing skills, you have saved me hours and hours, you are truly a wonderful friend.

Mary

INTRODUCTION

I would like to welcome you to my cookbook. I developed this cookbook because I found a need for recipes that were good for feeding my parents. Both of my parents had strokes, my Dad in 1990 and my Mom in 2003. Dad was ok eating regular food, but my Mom lost her ability to swallow after her stroke in 2003. Mom regained the ability to swallow in a few months, but she had to eat very soft foods so she couldn't just eat regular food. For example, a hamburger was out of the question for Mom. I searched high and low to find a cookbook that catered to soft foods and foods that fit into both of my parent's dietary restrictions as being low-salt and low sugar foods. I found a lot of recipes that would fit one of the categories, but not all three.

After many trials and tribulations with food types my sister, Anna ,and I decided that we would cook meals for our parents on the weekends and package them into small 2 serving portions and freeze them so our staff could just pop them in the oven and serve our parents. Download my e-book <u>Preparing Meals for the Elderly</u> to learn how to do this type of cooking.

I have put the number of servings so you can decide if you would like to double or triple these recipes if you are making ahead and freezing the meals. Most times we would triple them depending on the serving size.

All of these recipes can be made ahead and frozen. Feel free to swap out veggies and meats in the recipes, to make yet another new meal.

I have adapted recipes I found in cookbook, TV shows, internet sites, and meals I made on my own. I have removed all added salt, replaced eggs with egg substitutes, and added lots of spices that are not "hot" to increase the flavor of the recipes.

Mostly I use dry spices, but you certainly can use fresh, just remember you have to use a larger quantity of any fresh spice. We also used as much fresh veggies as possible, but you can't beat the frozen ones. They are very good and sometimes they can be better than fresh since they are flash frozen at their peak of freshness as opposed to veggies that have set on the shelf or in your fridge for a few weeks. Canned veggies can be high in salt (Sodium) so read the labels carefully if salt is a dietary restriction before using canned veggies.

I sometimes made my own soup stocks, but mostly I used the boxed low sodium ones or the ones marked "organic." If I just happened to have a turkey carcass hanging around after Thanksgiving or Christmas, you better believe I threw that puppy into a stock pot and got some free soup stock.

I hope that you enjoy these recipes and you find them useful. I have certainly enjoyed compiling them for you. If you purchased my e-book <u>Preparing Food for the Elderly</u> or any of my other e-books I want to thank you so much!!

Mary Davis

BEEF

My Sister Joan
At a home we rented for a family vacation

BEEF AND POTATO CASSEROLE
(Serves 6)

7 small baking potatoes, peeled and sliced
1 lb. ground beef
1 – 16 oz. pkg. frozen mixed vegetables, thawed
¼ teaspoon garlic powder
1 – 10.75 oz. can low salt condensed cream of mushroom soup
1 cup shredded Cheddar cheese
Pepper to taste

In a medium bowl, stir together the mixed vegetables, garlic powder and mushroom soup. Set aside.

Place the potatoes in a large saucepan with enough water to cover. Bring to a boil, and then simmer over medium heat until tender, about 5 minutes. Drain and set aside.

Meanwhile, crumble the ground beef into a large skillet over medium-high heat. Cook until evenly browned, stirring to break up large lumps. Drain excess grease from the beef and place in the bottom of a 9x13 inch baking dish. Pour the vegetable mixture over the beef, and then arrange the potato slices over the vegetables. Season with pepper. Sprinkle cheese over the top.

Bake uncovered for 25 minutes at 350 degrees until cheese is melted and the dish is heated through and bubbly.

WILD RICE AND BEEF CASSEROLE

(Serves 8)

3 cups chicken broth
¾ cup uncooked wild rice
1 ¼ cups uncooked brown rice
2 bay leaves
½ cup butter
1 medium onion, chopped
1 lb. ground beef
12 oz. sliced mushrooms
2 tsp. low sodium soy sauce
1 tsp. curry powder
2 cups shredded Cheddar cheese

In a medium pot, bring the chicken broth to a boil, and mix in the wild rice, brown rice, and bay leaves. Reduce heat to low, cover, and simmer 45 minutes, until most of the broth has been absorbed.

In a skillet, melt the butter and sauté onion until tender. Stir in the ground beef, and cook until evenly brown. Mix in the mushrooms, soy sauce, and curry powder, and continue to cook and stir until heated through.

Mix the beef mixture into the rice mixture, and remove the bay leaf. Transfer to a 9x13 inch baking dish. Top with Cheddar cheese.

Bake 20 minutes at 350 degrees, until bubbly and lightly browned.

SAUCY BEEF AND VEGETABLE CASSEROLE
(Serves 8)

1 lb. ground beef
1 cup shredded zucchini
1 small onion, chopped
1 clove garlic, minced
½ tsp. dried marjoram
½ cup salsa
1 – 10.75 oz. can low sodium condensed tomato soup
1 – 15 oz. can whole kernel corn, drained
1 cup frozen peas, thawed
2 cups cheddar cheese
Whole-wheat noodles

Lightly grease a 9x13 inch baking dish.

In a large skillet over medium heat, brown the ground beef. Drain the fat from the beef, and mix in the zucchini, onion, peas, garlic, and marjoram. Cook and stir until vegetables are tender. Mix in the salsa, tomato soup, and corn. Cook noodles according to package. Transfer noodles to the prepared baking dish and top with ground beef mixture. Top with cheddar cheese.

Bake covered in the preheated over 25 minutes at 375 degrees, or until the topping is golden brown.

BEEF AND ZUCCHINI CASSEROLE

(Serves 4 to 6)

4 cups thinly sliced zucchini
2 tbsp. oil
½ cup chopped onion
2 cloves garlic, minced
1 lb. lean ground beef
½ tsp. oregano
½ tsp. basil
¼ tsp. pepper
1 cup cooked rice
1 – 8 oz. can low sodium tomato sauce
1 cup ricotta cheese (low fat)
¾ cup shredded sharp Cheddar cheese
1 egg

Place half of the zucchini in a buttered 2 quart casserole. Heat oil in skillet; sauté onion and garlic until tender; add ground beef and cook until no longer pink. Drain off excess fat; add oregano, basil, and pepper to taste. Stir in rice and tomato sauce. Spread over zucchini in casserole. Combine ricotta cheese, ½ cup Cheddar cheese, and egg; spoon over meat mixture. Top with remaining zucchini and sprinkle with remaining Cheddar cheese. Bake in preheated 350 degree oven 20 to 25 minutes, or until bubbly.

ZUCCHINI PASTA CASSEROLE

(Serves 6-8)

1 lb. lean ground beef
1 ½ cups sliced onions
2 cups unpeeled, diced zucchini
2 tsp. finely chopped fresh garlic
2 – 28 oz. cans low sodium stewed or diced tomatoes with juice, chopped
2 tbsp. low sodium soy sauce
1 tsp crushed red pepper flakes
4 cups spiral-shaped pasta
2 cups shredded Cheddar cheese

Grease a large deep ovenproof casserole dish.

Brown meat with onions, zucchini, and garlic. Cook until meat is done and vegetables are soft. Drain fat. Mix in dry pasta.

In another bowl mix tomatoes and their juice, cheese, soy sauce, and red pepper flakes. Mix into beef mixture. Put mixture into prepared dish, ensuring that the pasta is submerged in the liquid. Bake for 50 minutes at 350 degrees.

LEFTOVER MEAT AND POTATO CASSEROLE

(Serves 4)

2 cups sliced onions
1 tsp. sugar
1 tbsp. butter
3 cups seasoned mashed potatoes
8 slices pot roast, roast beef, pork roast, or meatloaf
1 cup frozen peas, thawed
1 can beef gravy, about 10 ½ oz. or 1 cup leftover gravy
¼ cup shredded mild Cheddar cheese

Put onions in a non-stick skillet sprinkle with sugar and fry over medium heat, stirring, until onions begin to brown. Add butter and cook until onions are tender, about 7 minutes. Remove from heat. Spread half of the mashed potatoes into a greased, 2-quart shallow baking dish. Arrange slices of meat on top, then onions, peas, and gravy. Cover with remaining mashed potatoes. Bake at 375 degrees for 30 minutes; top with shredded cheese and bake 10 minutes longer, or until casserole is browned and cheese is melted.

GROUND BEEF CASSEROLE
(Serves 6)

1 lb. lean ground beef
1 cup chopped onion
1 cup green bell pepper
1 – 15 ½ oz. can diced low sodium tomatoes
1 tbsp. Worcestershire sauce
1 can whole kernel corn, drained
2 cups thinly sliced potatoes (slightly cooked)
½ cup flour
1 ½ cups shredded mild Cheddar or American cheese

Peel potatoes if you choose to and cut into small pieces. Boil for 5 minutes so they are partially cooked but not completely cooked. Allow to cool. You can use raw potatoes, but do not freeze casserole; you must cook it right away. If you freeze uncooked potatoes they will blacken.

Combine beef, onion, tomatoes, and Worcestershire sauce. In a separate bowl, combine corn, potatoes, flour, and chopped green bell pepper.

Place beef mixture in a shallow casserole or baking dish in layers with corn and potato mixture.

Bake uncovered a 375 degrees for 45 minutes; then sprinkle with cheese and bake ground beef casserole 30 minutes longer, or until vegetables are done.

EASY GROUND BEEF CASSEROLE WITH POTATOES

(Serves 4 to 6)

1 – 1 ½ lb. lean ground beef, browned
½ cup chopped onion
Pepper
¼ teaspoon garlic powder
3 large potatoes, sliced and parboiled
2 carrots, shredded
1 can cream of mushroom soup
1 cup shredded Cheddar cheese

Peel potatoes if you choose to and cut into small pieces. Boil for 5 minutes so they are partially cooked but not completely cooked. Allow to cool. You can use raw potatoes, but do not freeze casserole; you must cook it right away. If you freeze uncooked potatoes they will blacken.

Place ground beef in a skillet with chopped onions and garlic powder; cook until onions are tender. Drain off excess fat; transfer ground beef and onion to casserole dish. Add layer of sliced potatoes, sprinkle with pepper; shred carrots to cover potatoes. Put soup over carrots. Bake at 350 degrees for 40 to 50 minutes, or until potatoes are tender. Sprinkle shredded cheese over top and bake for about 5 minutes longer, or until cheese is melted.

GROUND BEEF CASSEROLE WITH RICE

(Serves 4)

Pepper
Paprika
1 cup chopped onion
3 medium potatoes sliced
1 ¼ lb. lean ground beef
2 cups **cooked** long grain rice
1 cup chopped carrots
1 cup chopped celery
1 can low sodium tomato soup
1/2 cup boiling water

Peel potatoes if you choose to and cut into small pieces. Boil for 5 minutes so they are partially cooked but not completely cooked. Allow to cool. You can use raw potatoes, but do not freeze casserole; you must cook it right away. If you freeze uncooked potatoes they will blacken.

Butter a 2 ½ quart casserole dish. Sprinkling each layer with salt, peppers, and paprika, layer the casserole with the onions, potatoes, ground beef, rice, carrots, and celery. Combine condensed soup with the boiling water and pour over casserole. Bake at 300 degrees for 1 hour.

SEVEN LAYER CASSEROLE WITH GROUND BEEF

(Serves 6)

1 cup uncooked rice, washed and drained
1 cup whole kernel corn, drained
Dash salt and pepper
1 – 8 oz. can low sodium tomato sauce and ½ cup water
½ cup chopped onion
¾ to 1 lb. extra lean ground beef, uncooked and broken up
Dash salt and pepper
1 – 14.5 oz. can diced no salt tomatoes, with juice
4 strips bacon, cut in half
Shredded cheese, if desired for topping

Place ingredients in a buttered 1 ½ quart casserole dish in order given. Cover and bake at 350 degrees for 1 hour. Uncover and cook 30 minutes longer, until bacon is crisp. If desired, top with shredded cheese the last 10 to 15 minutes.

Mom and Anna St. George Island July 2003

TEXAS BEAN BAKE

(Serves 6)

1 – 16 oz. can pork and beans
1 – 16 oz. can red kidney beans
1 – 16 oz. can pinto beans
8 slices bacon, cooked crisp, crumbled
1 lb. lean ground beef
1 chopped onion
1 tbsp. prepared mustard
1 cup chopped carrots
1 ½ cups ketchup
¼ cup brown sugar
¼ cup white sugar

Brown the ground beef with chopped onion. Combine all ingredients, except bacon, in a large casserole dish. Top with the crumbled bacon. Bake at 350 degrees for about 1 hour.

RICE MINESTRONE SOUP

(Serves 5)

2 Tbs. olive oil
1 onion, finely chopped
1 red bell pepper, chopped
1 carrot, chopped
1 potato, peeled and chopped
1 zucchini, chopped
1 yellow squash, chopped
1 eggplant, chopped
½ cup rice
2-14 oz. cans Italian tomatoes, diced
1 stalk broccoli, chopped
½ cup frozen baby peas, thawed
1 lb ground beef
6 cups low sodium beef broth
Parmesan cheese

Heat the olive oil in pan and add the beef, onion and red bell pepper and cook over moderately high heat stirring occasionally until softened and lightly browned. Drain fat from pan. Add the carrots, potatoes, zucchini, yellow squash, and eggplant and cook stirring often for 5 minutes.

Add the rice to the saucepan and toss well to coat the greens with oil. Add the tomatoes, ¼ teaspoon black pepper, and six cups of beef broth and bring to a boil over moderately high heat. Add the broccoli and peas and cook stirring until all the vegetables and rice are tender, about 35 minutes. Serve. Garnish with Parmesan cheese.

ITALIAN WEDDING SOUP

(Serves 8)

Meatballs
1 small onion, grated
1/3 cup chopped fresh Italian parsley
1 large egg
1 tsp. minced garlic
1 slice fresh white bread, crust trimmed, bread torn into small pieces
½ cup grated Parmesan cheese
8 oz. ground beef
8 oz. ground pork
Freshly ground black pepper

Soup
12 cups low-sodium chicken broth
1 lb. curly endive, coarsely chopped
2 large eggs
2 tbsp. freshly grated Parmesan, plus extra for garnish
Black pepper

To make the meatballs, stir the first 5 ingredients in a large bowl to blend. Stir in the cheese, beef and pork. Using 1 ½ teaspoons for each, shape the meat mixture into 1-inch diameter meatballs. In a large soup pan, add a little olive oil or vegetable cooking spray and brown the meatballs. Drain fat from pan.

Add the broth to the pot and bring to a boil. Add curly endive and simmer until the curly endive is tender. Whisk the eggs and cheese in a medium bowl to blend. Stir the soup in a circular motion. Gradually drizzle the egg mixture into the moving broth, stirring gently with a fork to form thin stands of egg, about 1 minute. Season the soup to taste with salt and pepper.

Ladle the soup into bowls and serve. Finish soup with Parmesan cheese, if desired.

WALDORF STEW – CROCK POT

(Serves 6 to 8)

2 lb. beef, sirloin cut up raw
2 cups potatoes cut in pieces
2 cups carrots cut in pieces
2 cups celery cut in pieces
2 cups green beans cut in pieces
1 – 16 oz. can low sodium diced tomatoes, with juice
2 tbsp. dry minced onion
3 tbsp. quick cooking tapioca
1 tbsp. sugar
1 can low sodium tomato soup
Pepper to taste

Place all in a large crock pot. Cover and cook at low setting for 5 hours. Do not stir. Add any additional vegetables you like.

BARLEY SOUP FOR A CROCK POT

(Serves 6)

1 lb. stew beef, cut in ½-inch cubes
1 medium onion, chopped
2 stalks celery, chopped
2 carrots, diced
2/4 cups barley
1 bay leaf
Pepper to taste
6 cups low sodium beef stock
1 tea ball (bottom) almost full of Herbs de Province

Cook on low in crock pot for 6 to 8 hours stirring occasionally. Remove bay leaf and tea ball before serving.

FRONTIER STEW

(Serves 6-8)

1 1/2 lb. ground beef
1 medium onion, peeled and chopped
¼ cup green bell pepper, seeded and chopped
1 clove garlic, peeled and minced
¼ cup chopped celery
1 tbsp. chili powder
¼ tsp. granulated sugar
Black pepper to taste
1 – 16 oz. can low sodium diced tomatoes, undrained
1 – 16 oz. can whole kernel corn, undrained
1 – 32 oz. can ranch-style beans, undrained
6 medium potatoes, peeled and cubed
3 cups water

Brown ground beef in pan. Add onion, green pepper, garlic, and celery; cook until vegetables are soft. Add chili powder, sugar, and pepper; mix well. Add tomatoes with their liquid, corn, beans, potatoes, and water. Bring to a boil stirring well. Reduce heat. Cover and simmer until potatoes are tender. Stir occasionally during cooking.

NOTE: Ranch-style beans are spicy pinto beans they are available in many supermarkets across the country. If not available, use any brand of canned pinto beans and, if desired, add chopped green chilies, if desired.

PACKER STEW

(Serves 8)

2 to 2 ½ lb. round steak, trimmed and cut into small pieces
1 – 17 oz. can peas, drained
1 small onion, chopped
4 tbsp. tapioca
8 oz. mushrooms, chopped and drained
1 ½ to 2 cups carrots, diced
2 cloves garlic, minced
3 to 4 large potatoes, diced
1 – 28 oz. can low sodium diced tomatoes
1 cup celery, chopped
1 tsp. granulated sugar
1 green bell pepper, chopped
Pepper to taste

Combine all ingredients in a crock pot. Cook on high for 5 hours.

BOY SCOUT COWBOY STEW

(Serves 8)

1 lb. ground beef
1 – 28 oz. can low sodium stewed tomatoes, diced
2 – 15 ¼ oz. can whole kernel corn
2 – 15 oz. cans whole green beans
1 – 15 ½ oz. can red beans, drained and rinsed
1 onion, chopped
½ tsp. dried oregano
¼ tsp. cayenne pepper
Pepper to taste

Brown the ground beef in a skillet. Drain off any excess grease. In a stockpot or Dutch oven, combine ground beef, tomatoes, corn green beans, red beans, and onion. Season with oregano, cayenne pepper, and pepper to taste. Cover and simmer for at least 50 minutes over medium to low heat. The longer this cooks the better flavor it has. This recipe can be cooked in crock pot for 6 hours on high.

WASTEBASKET SOUP

(Serves 8 to 10)

1 ½ lb. beef stew meat, cut into 1-inch cubes
1 chopped onion
2 tbsp. olive oil
1 tsp. minced garlic
8 cups low sodium beef broth
1 ½ tsp. dried Italian seasoning
1 – 15 oz. can great northern beans or navy beans, rinsed and drained
1 – 14 ½ oz. can low sodium tomatoes, cut up
1 ½ cups thinly sliced carrots
2 cups sliced zucchini
1 cup dried small pasta shells
Grated Parmesan cheese (optional)

In a frying pan, brown beef, onion, oil, and garlic. Remove fat from pan. Put beef mixture into crock pot. Add broth, Italian seasoning, beans, tomatoes, and carrots. Cover and cook 6 hours on high. Stir in zucchini and pasta and cook 1 hour on high or until pasta is tender. Sprinkle each serving with Parmesan cheese, if desired.

Jerry, Aaron, Kelley, and Sam Camping

CIDER BEEF STEW RECIPE

(Serves 6)

1 – 2 lb. beef stew meat
8 carrots, sliced thin
6 potatoes, sliced thin
2 apples, chopped
½ tsp. thyme
2 tbsp. minced onion
2 cups apple cider

Place carrots, potatoes, and apples in crock pot. Add meat and sprinkle with thyme and onion. Pour cider over meat and cover. Cook on low heat 10 to 12 hours. Thicken gravy with a flour or cornstarch and water mixture.

MEATLOAF

(Serves 8)

3 slices bread
1 large carrot, peeled and cut into ¼-inch pieces
1 rib celery, cut into ½-inch pieces
½ medium yellow onion, peeled and roughly chopped
2 cloves garlic, smashed and peeled
½ cup flat leaf parsley leaves, loosely packed
½ cup plus 3 tbsp. ketchup
4 ½ tsp. liquid mustard
8 oz. ground pork
8 oz. ground round
8 oz. ground turkey
½ lb. bacon, added to meats
2 large eggs, beaten
1/3 lb. Swiss cheese
1 tsp. ground black pepper
¼ tsp. Cajun seasoning such as Tony Chachere's
½ tsp. chopped fresh rosemary plus needles for sprinkling
2 tbsp. dark brown sugar
1 tbsp. olive oil
1 small red onion, cut into ¼-inch thick rings
1 cup diced mushrooms

Heat oven to 400 degrees. Remove crusts from bread and place in the bowl of a food processor. Process until fine crumbs form about 10 seconds. Transfer breadcrumbs to a large mixing bowl. Do not substitute dried breadcrumbs in this step as they will make your meatloaf rubbery.

Place carrot, celery, yellow onion, garlic and parsley in the bowl of the food processor. Process till vegetables have been minced about 30 seconds, stopping to scrape down the sides of the bowl once or twice. Transfer vegetables to bowl with the breadcrumbs.

Add ½ cup ketchup, 2 tsp. liquid mustard, pork, turkey, beef, eggs, pepper, bacon, Cajun seasoning, and rosemary. Using your hands, knead the ingredients until thoroughly combined about one minute. Do not over knead. The texture should be wet, but tight enough to hold a free-form shape.

Set a wire baking rack into an 11x17 inch baking pan. Cut a 5x11 inch piece of parchment paper and place over center of rack to prevent meatloaf from falling through. Using your hands form an elongated meatloaf covering the parchment.

Place the remaining 3 tbsp. ketchup, remaining 2 ½ tsp. liquid mustard, and brown sugar in a bowl. Mix until smooth. Using a pastry brush, generously brush the glaze over meatloaf. Place oil in a medium saucepan set over high heat. When oil is smoking add red onion. Cook stirring occasionally until onion is soft and golden in places. Add 3 tbsp. water, and cook stirring until most of water has evaporated Transfer onion to a bowl to cool slightly then sprinkle onion over the meatloaf.

Bake 30 minutes then sprinkle rosemary needles on top. Continue baking loaf until an instant read thermometer inserted into the center of the meatloaf registers 160 degrees, about 25 minutes more. Let meatloaf cool on rack, about 15 minutes.

Quinn and Andy (Mom & Dad's 1st grandson)

CHICKEN

Jerry, Joan, Ed, Ellie, Mary, Anna
Aunt Jay
At Mom and Dad's home in Florida before Mom's stroke

MONDAY CHICKEN
(Serves 4)

4 skinless, boneless chicken breast halves
1 (14 ounce) bag frozen broccoli florets
1 (10.75 ounce) can condensed golden mushroom soup
1/3 cup sour cream (light or no-fat)
1 tablespoon prepared horseradish (optional)

Preheat the oven to 350 degrees F (175 degrees C). Spray a 9x13 inch baking dish with cooking spray. Spread the broccoli evenly in the bottom of the baking dish or individual serving dishes. Place chicken breasts over the broccoli.

In a medium bowl, stir together the condensed soup, sour cream and horseradish. Pour or spread evenly over the chicken and broccoli. Bake uncovered for 1 hour in the preheated oven. Let stand for a few minutes before serving for the sauce to thicken.

LEFTOVER CHICKEN CASSEROLE

(Serves 6)

4 large potatoes, peeled and sliced
3 med. onions, sliced
1 can peas, drained
1 can mushroom soup (low sodium), diluted with milk
Leftover chicken (or turkey)

In casserole dish or individual serving dishes, place a layer of potatoes and layer of onion slices. Sprinkle some of the peas over the layer. Next, add pieces of chicken. Continue this until casserole is 3/4 full. Pour over the layers the mushroom soup. Place in a preheated oven (350 degrees) until the potatoes are tender.

For a variation, try sweet potatoes instead of the regular ones!

CHICKEN WITH POMEGRANATE SAUCE

(Serves 6-8)

3 lbs chicken cut into small pieces
4 cups walnuts
4 red onions
Hot water
2 tablespoons olive oil
2 ½ cups pomegranate juice
2 tablespoons ground cardamom
2 tablespoons cinnamon
1 butternut squash seeded and cubed
Cooked rice

Peel onions and slice thinly. Fry in oil until slightly golden. Wash chicken pieces and fry in onions until color changes. Add 3 glasses of hot water and bring to boil. Turn heat down and let boil slowly for about 30 minutes adding more hot water if needed.

Combine the walnuts and pomegranate juice in a food processor or blender. Add blended mixture to the simmering chicken. Add cardamom, cinnamon and a dash of salt and stir in the squash. Transfer to a baking dish or individual serving dishes. Bake at 325 degrees for 2 ½ hours or until squash is soft.

Serve over rice

CHICKEN-HAM-SHRIMP CASSEROLE

(Serves 6)

3/4 c. butter
3/4 c. flour
1/4 tsp. salt
1/4 tsp. pepper
3 c. milk
4 c. grated Cheddar cheese
3 c. sherry (optional)
4 c. cooked diced chicken
2 c. cooked diced ham (don't use lunch meat ham – way too salty)
1 (24 oz.) pkg. frozen shrimp, cooked
1 (8 oz.) pkg. wide noodles, cooked according to pkg. directions for noodles used in casseroles (al dente) hint: use "no egg" noodles if watching cholesterol.

Make white sauce of butter, flour, salt, pepper and milk. Add cheese, stirring until melted. Remove from heat and stir in sherry. Add chicken, ham, shrimp and noodles. Pour into greased baking dish or individual serving dishes and bake, covered, 35 minutes in 350 degree oven.

HINT: To make ham less salty boil ham in water for 20 minutes and drain. If still salty, boil again.

SWEET POTATO CHICKEN CASSEROLE

(Serves 6)

1 tablespoon olive oil
1 large onion, finely chopped
1 clove garlic, chopped
2 pounds sweet potatoes, peeled and diced
2 carrots, diced
2 cups frozen veggies of your choice (mixed, peas, green beans, broccoli etc)
4 skinless, boneless chicken breast halves - diced
2 tablespoons all-purpose flour
1 cup dry white wine (optional)
2 cups low sodium chicken stock

Heat the oil in a large skillet over medium heat. Add the onion and garlic, and cook until just starting to turn golden. Mix in the sweet potatoes and carrot; cook and stir for a few minutes, until lightly browned.

Add the chicken; cook and stir until seared on all sides. Scatter the flour over the top, and stir it in. Gradually stir in the chicken stock, mixing carefully so that no flour lumps form. Scrape any bits of food from the bottom of the pan while you do this. Pour in the wine last, and mix thoroughly. Transfer to a casserole dish or individual serving dishes and cover with a lid or tin foil and bake for 1 hour at 400 degrees.

CHICKEN AND PEA CASSEROLE

(Serves 6-8)

1 (16 ounce) package pasta of your choice
1 can low sodium cream of mushroom soup
3/4 cup sour cream (light or no-fat)
1 lb diced cooked chicken
1 cup frozen peas, thawed
1 1/2 teaspoons garlic powder
2 1/2 teaspoons onion powder
½ teaspoon Creole seasoning (like Tony's Chachere's)
1/2 teaspoon black pepper
2 cups grated Parmesan cheese

Bring a large pot of water to a boil. Add 1/2 teaspoon salt and pasta, and cook until almost done and drain.

In a large bowl, stir together mushroom soup, sour cream, chicken, and peas. Season with garlic powder, onion powder, Creole seasoning, and pepper

Stir cooked pasta into chicken mixture until well combined. Pour pasta mixture into a 9x10-inch casserole dish or individual serving dishes, and spread out evenly. Top with Parmesan cheese, and spray the top with a bit of cooking spray.

Bake in a preheated oven until golden brown, about 20 to 25 minutes. Remove from oven, and let cool 5 minutes.

CHICKEN AND RICE BAKE

(Serves 4)

1 cup long-grain rice, uncooked
1 cup celery
1 ½ cups frozen peas
1 ½ cups frozen green beans
2 cups low sodium chicken broth
2 tablespoons butter
2 cups cooked diced chicken
2 tablespoons flour
1/8 teaspoon pepper
1 teaspoon garlic powder
2/3 cup evaporated milk
1 cup shredded cheese or American cheese

In a medium saucepan, combine rice, celery, chicken broth and bring to a boil. Cover and simmer for about 8 minutes; add peas and beans and cook an additional 8 to 10 minutes or until rice is tender and water is absorbed.

Melt butter in a medium saucepan or skillet. Sauté chicken for about 1 minute then stir in flour, garlic and pepper. Continue to cook, stirring constantly, just until bubbling. Stir in milk and 1 1/3 cups water. Continue cooking and stirring until sauce thickens and gently boils for about 1 minute. Pour sauce over the chicken rice mixture; transfer to shallow buttered 2-quart baking dish or individual serving dishes. Sprinkle with cheese; bake at 375° for 20 minutes.

MARY'S CHICKEN FLORENTINE

(Serves 6-8)

2 packages (10 ounces each) frozen chopped spinach
1/4 cup butter
Clove garlic, crushed and mince
Dash dried basil
Dash ground thyme
1/4 cup all-purpose flour
1/3 cup half-and-half or whipping cream
5 cups cooked chicken, sliced
3 cups frozen veggies of your choice
3/4 cup half-and-half or whipping cream
3/4 cup low sodium chicken broth
Dash pepper
6 thin slices ham
1 cup grated Parmesan cheese
1 package noodles of your choice cooked al dente according to package directions.

Cook spinach according to package instructions, drain well. In a skillet, melt 1 tablespoon butter; add minced garlic, basil, and thyme. Cook over medium low heat, stirring constantly, for about 5 minutes

Add 1 tablespoon flour and blend well. Add 1/3 cup half-and-half and the spinach; simmer for 5 minutes, stirring constantly. Put spinach and noodles into the bottom of a lightly buttered 2-quart casserole or baking dish or individual serving dishes. Cover with cooked chicken slices. Over medium low heat, melt remaining butter and blend in remaining flour, stirring until smooth. Gradually stir in 3/4 cup half-and-half and 3/4 cup chicken broth; continue cooking and stirring until thickened. Season to taste with pepper. Cut sliced ham in strips. Add to sauce and pour over chicken. Cover all with grated Parmesan cheese. Bake at 400° for 20 minutes, or until cheese is lightly browned.

CHIKEN NOODLE CASSEROLE

(Serves 6)

8 oz. Wide Egg Noodles, uncooked or "no yokes"
1/2 cup non-fat sour cream
1 cup low-sodium chicken broth
2 tbsp. grated Parmesan cheese
1/2 cup egg substitute
2 tbsp. Dijon mustard
1 1/2 cups chopped broccoli, blanched and drained
1 1/2 cups skinless, boneless chicken breast, cooked

Topping
2 tbsp. bread crumbs
2 tablespoons Parmesan cheese
1 tablespoon Italian Seasoning

Prepare egg noodles according to package directions; drain. Whisk the sour cream, chicken broth, 2 tablespoons of the Parmesan cheese, eggs and mustard in a bowl until blended. Add noodles, broccoli and chicken and toss well. Transfer the mixture to a 9 x 12-inch baking dish.

In a bowl add 2 tablespoons Parmesan cheese, Italian Seasoning and bread crumbs stir together and sprinkle over casserole. Bake uncovered at 350 until bubbling around the edges and the top is golden brown, about 35 minutes. Let stand 5 minutes before serving.

CHICKEN FETTUCCINE WITH LIGHT ALFREDO SAUCE

(Serves 4)

1 pound Fettuccine, Linguine or Spaghetti, uncooked
1 cup evaporated skim milk
1 pound cooked diced chicken
½ cup chopped fresh parsley
¼ tsp. white pepper
½ cup grated Parmesan cheese
4 oz. green onions, sliced (white parts only)
White pepper to taste

Prepare pasta according to package directions; drain. In a large sauce pan, bring the evaporated milk to a simmer over moderate heat. Stir in the Parmesan cheese, chicken, green onions and parsley. As soon as it has melted, and the sauce is thick and creamy, pour over cooked pasta. Season to taste with white pepper.

OVERNIGHT CHICKEN ITALIANO

(Serves 4)

1 – 2 ½ to 3 lb. frying chicken
1/3 cup oil (half olive oil and half corn oil)
1/4 cup vinegar
½ Lemon (juice only)
1 tsp. garlic powder
½ cup grated Romano cheese
½ cup dry bread crumbs
Salt and pepper
Cooked noodles of your choice

Cut chicken into serving pieces. Marinate chicken overnight in oil, vinegar, lemon juice, and garlic powder. Next day, place chicken in baking pan and sprinkle lightly with cheese, bread crumbs, salt and pepper. Cover pan loosely with foil and bake at 350 degrees for 45 minutes or until tender. Serve with cooked noodles seasoned only with garlic and butter.

LINGUINE CHEESE ALMANDINE

(Serves 4 – 6)

½ cup slivered almonds, blanched
1 cup low-fat cottage cheese
½ tsp. Italian herb seasoning
¼ cup sliced green onions
2 tbsp. milk
1 cup chicken broth
2 tbsp. grated Parmesan cheese
1 cup frozen peas, thawed
2 tbsp. butter
8 oz. linguine, cooked to package direction
Freshly ground pepper to taste
Grated Parmesan cheese for garnish

Preheat oven to 350 degrees. Toast almonds on a cookie sheet in the oven for 5 – 7 minutes. Remove from oven and set aside. In bowl, combine cottage cheese, Italian herbs, onion, milk, chicken broth, Parmesan cheese and peas. Stir well. Set aside. Heat butter in a skillet over medium heat. Add cooked and drained linguine. Stir to mix well. While linguine is warm, add cheese mixture and stir gently until heated. Stir in pepper; top with toasted almonds and serve immediately. Serve with Parmesan cheese.

CROCKPOT CHICKEN CACCIATORE

(Serves 6)

1 - 2 ½ to 3 lb. chicken (remove skin)
1 can stewed tomatoes – No Salt added
1 can tomato sauce
2 cloves garlic, diced
1 medium onion, diced
2 stalks of celery, chopped
1 tsp. oregano
½ tsp. sweet basil
½ tsp. rosemary
½ tsp. cilantro
¼ tsp. pepper
1 zucchini squash cut into pieces
1 yellow squash cut into pieces

Mix stewed tomatoes, tomato sauce; add rest of ingredients. Mix well. Pour over chicken and turn crock pot on high until mixture begins to boil. Turn down on low and let simmer for the day (8 hours). Serve over pasta or rice. Freezes well.

SCALLOPED CHICKEN

(Serves 6-8)

3 tbsp. butter
3 tbsp. flour
2 cups chicken broth
1 cup skim milk
1 cup frozen peas (thawed)
3 cups cooked rice
3 cups cooked diced chicken
2 cups sliced sautéed mushrooms
½ cup slivered almonds

Melt butter over low heat in a medium saucepan; stir in flour, blending well. Add chicken broth, milk, salt, and pepper. Cook stirring constantly until thickened. Butter a 2-quart baking dish. Spread half of the rice in the bottom of the baking dish; top with half of the chicken, half of the sliced mushrooms, half of the slivered almonds. Pour in half of the sauce. Repeat layers; sprinkle with buttered bread crumbs. Bake at 350 degrees for 45 minutes.

ZUCCHINI, CHICKEN, AND RICE CASSEROLE

(Serves 6)

4 tbsp. vegetable oil, divided
2 cups onion, chopped
1 garlic clove, minced
3 cups zucchini, diced
2 cups mushrooms, sliced
1 cup frozen peas (thawed)
3 cups chicken, cooked and diced
1 cup cooked brown or white rice
2 ½ cups low sodium chicken broth or water
1 ½ tsp. fresh thyme (or ½ tsp. dried)
½ tsp. rosemary
½ cup grated Parmesan cheese
Pepper
2 cups tomatoes – (no salt added if canned), chopped
¼ tsp. chili powder

Heat 3 tbsp. of the oil in a large sauté pan, and sauté 1 cup of the onions with the garlic for 2 minutes. Add the zucchini, peas and mushrooms, and sauté for 3 minutes more. Combine the vegetables with the chicken, rice, broth, spices, and cheese. Season to taste with pepper. Place this mixture in a greased 9x13 baking dish.

Heat the remaining 1 tbsp. oil and sauté the remaining cup of onions for 3 minutes. Add the tomatoes and chili powder. Spoon the topping over the rice and chicken mixture. Bake at 350 degrees for 1 hour.

CHICKEN CORDON BLUE CASSEROLE

(Serves 6-8)

2 lbs. skinless chicken breasts cut into chunks
Italian Bread Crumbs
1 egg
½ cup milk
8 oz. Swiss cheese, cubed
8 oz. ham, diced
1 can (10 ¾ oz.) cream of chicken soup
1 cup milk
2 cups green beans
Cooked noodles of your choice

Whisk together the egg and ½ cup milk. Dip chunks of chicken in egg mixture, then into bread crumbs, coating well. Brown in peanut or olive oil until golden brown.

Place cooked noodles and chicken pieces in baking dish; add cubes of Swiss cheese and small pieces of ham. Mix cream of chicken soup with 1 cup of milk; mix well and pour over all. Bake about 30 minutes at 350 degrees or until tender and bubbly.

SOUTHERN CHICKEN CASSEROLE

(Serves 8-10)

1 – 3 to 4 lb. chicken
3 ¼ cups water
Few sprigs parsley
1 stalk celery, chopped
1 cup onion, chopped and divided
¼ tsp. dried leaf thyme
1 pkg. (10 oz.) frozen corn, thawed
1 pkg. (10 oz.) frozen French-cut green beans, thawed
3 tbsp. cornstarch
¼ cup butter
3 cups coarse soft bread crumbs
1 egg, beaten
½ tsp. ground sage
Pepper, to taste
Cooked noodles of your choice

In a large Dutch oven or stock pot, combine chicken, water, parsley, celery, half of the onions, and thyme. Cover and cook chicken until very tender, about 1 ¼ hours. Drain reserving stock. Cool chicken. Then skin, bone, and chop meat. Strain stock.

Spread corn and green beans and noodles in a buttered 9x13 baking pan. Arrange chicken over the vegetables. Combine cornstarch and reserved stock in a medium saucepan and stir until dissolved. Bring to a boil, stirring constantly. Pour sauce over chicken.

Preheat over to 325 degrees.

Melt butter in a small saucepan. Add remaining ½ cup of onions and cook over low heat until soft. In a medium bowl toss bread crumbs with butter and onions, the beaten egg, sage, and pepper. Sprinkle brad crumb mixture over chicken and bake for 25 minutes or until sauce is bubbly and top is browned.

CHICKEN AND WILD RICE CASSEROLE

(Serves 6)

3 cups cooked, chopped chicken breasts
1 pkg. quick cooking wild rice, cooked according to package directions
1 pkg. frozen French green beans, thawed and drained
2 tbsp. butter
¼ teaspoon garlic powder
1 teaspoon Italian seasoning
½ cup chopped onion
3 tbsp. flour
1 cup chicken stock
½ cup cream or milk
½ cup grated Parmesan cheese
¼ cup slivered almonds

In a buttered casserole dish, combine chicken, cooked rice and green beans. In a saucepan melt butter over medium high heat. Stir in onions and cook for 1 minute. Stir in flour and cook for 1 minute. Whisk in chicken stock and bring to a simmer. Whisk in cream or milk garlic, Italian seasoning and return to a simmer. When sauce has thickened, pour over mixture in casserole dish. Sprinkle with Parmesan cheese and almonds and bake for 30 minutes at 350 degrees.

FAMILY CASSEROLE

(Serves 6)

¼ cup butter or margarine
1 onion, chopped
2 stalks celery, chopped
1 – 10.75 oz. can low sodium condensed cream of celery soup
¼ cup low sodium chicken broth
1 – 16 oz. pkg. frozen chopped broccoli, thawed
1 – 5 oz. can water chestnuts, drained and sliced
2 cups cooked rice
2 cups cooked, cubed chicken meat
8 oz. Sliced mushrooms
½ tsp. garlic powder, or to taste
1 cup shredded Cheddar cheese

Melt butter in a large skillet over medium heat. Sauté the onion and celery until tender. Stir in the condensed soup and chicken broth. Add the broccoli, water chestnuts, rice, chicken, and mushrooms. Cook and stir briefly. Season with garlic powder. Mix in Cheddar cheese, and pour the mixture into a 9x13 inch baking dish. Bake for 30 minutes at 325 degrees, until heated through and bubbly.

AUTUMN PUMPKIN SOUP

(Serves 10 to 12)

1 lb. onions, chopped
3 cups sliced fresh mushrooms
½ cup (1 stick) butter
½ cup flour
2 quarts low sodium chicken stock
1 – 14 oz. can pumpkin
1 ½ tsp. curry powder
Pepper to taste
½ cup half-and-half
2 tbsp. honey
3 cups cooked chicken cut into small cubes

Sauté the onions and mushrooms in ¼ cup of the butter in a large saucepan until the onions are tender. Transfer the undrained onion mixture to a bowl. Heat the remaining ¼ cup butter in the same saucepan until melted. Add the flour and mix well. Whisk in the stock gradually.

Cook until thickened, stirring constantly. Stir in the onion mixture, pumpkin, curry powder, chicken and pepper. Add the half-and-half and honey and mix well. Cook just until heated through, stirring frequently. Ladle into soup bowls. Garnish each serving with a dollop of sour cream and minced fresh parsley. Serve with hot crusty French bread.

CHICKEN STEW WITH HERBS AND BARLEY

(Serves 6)

2 oz. butter
1 lb. Cubed chicken
1 lb. leeks, thickly sliced
4 cloves garlic, finely chopped
6 oz. barley
3 ¾ cups water
3 tbsp. wine vinegar
2 bay leaves
Pepper to taste
1 tbsp. dried sage

Melt the butter in a heavy pan and fry the meat with the leeks and garlic till the vegetables are slightly softened and the meat lightly browned. Add the barley, water, vinegar, bay leaves and seasoning, bring the pot to a boil, cover it and simmer gently for 1 to 1 ½ hours or till the meat is really tender. Add the sage and continue to cook for several minutes. Adjust the seasoning to taste and serve in bowls – the barley will serve as a vegetable.

Mary and Jerry - Wedding Day (6/27/99)

THAI-STYLE COCONUT-CHICKEN SOUP

(Serves 6)

1 lb. skinless, boneless chicken breasts cut into ¾-inch pieces
4 cups low sodium chicken broth
2 cups sliced carrots
2 tbsp. grated fresh ginger
¼ tsp. Cajun Spice such as Tony's Chachere's
3 cloves garlic, minced
3 – 15 oz. cans unsweetened coconut milk
1 medium red, yellow, and/or green sweet pepper, cut into ½-inch pieces
2 – 4 oz. cans straw or button mushrooms, drained
1 cup frozen peas
2 ribs celery cut into small pieces
1 medium zucchini cut into small cubes
1 medium yellow squash cut into small cubes
1 package small soup noodles of your choice
1/3 cup dry roasted chopped peanuts (optional)

In a 3 ½ to 5 quart slow cooker combine the chicken, broth, vegetables, ginger, garlic, and spices.

Cover; cook on low heat for 6 to 7 hours or on high heat for 3 to 3 /12 hours. If necessary, skim off fat. Stir coconut milk, sweet pepper, noodles and mushrooms into chicken mixture. Cover; and cook one hour on high. Ladle soup into bowls. Sprinkle peanuts over each serving if desired.

CHICKEN MEATBALL AND NOODLE SOUP

(Serves 8)

1 ½ cup Italian bread crumbs
¼ cup milk
4 cloves garlic, minced
1 tbsp. olive oil
1 ½ tsp. Worcestershire sauce
¼ tsp. freshly ground black pepper
1 large egg, slightly beaten
12 oz. uncooked ground chicken breast
1/3 cup grated Parmesan cheese
2 tbsp. snipped fresh flat-leaf parsley
3 tbsp. butter
4 stalks celery, chopped
3 medium carrots, chopped
1 large onion, chopped
½ tsp. freshly ground black pepper
10 cups reduced-sodium chicken broth
¾ cup dried alphabet-shape pasta

For meatballs combine bread crumbs, milk, garlic, oil, Worcestershire sauce, and the ¼ teaspoon black pepper in a large bowl. Add egg, ground chicken, Parmesan cheese, and parsley; mix well. Shape meat mixture into meatballs, each about 1 inch in diameter. Arrange meatballs in a 15x10x1-inch baking pan.

Bake in a 350 degrees oven for 12 to 15 minutes or until cooked through or you may pan the meatballs (I think you get a little better flavor by pan frying). Drain off fat. Set meatballs aside. (Meatballs can be made ahead and stored in a covered container overnight in the refrigerator or frozen for up to 3 months.)

For soup melt butter in a large Dutch oven or stockpot over medium-low heat. Add celery, carrots, onion, and the ½ teaspoon black pepper. Cook vegetables for 10 minutes, stirring frequently. Carefully add broth. Simmer covered for 20 minutes.

Add uncooked pasta; cook uncovered for 5 minutes. Add meatballs to soup; cook about 5 minutes more or until heated through and pasta is tender.

SUMMER MINESTRONI

(Serves 8)

2 cups mixed aromatic vegetables (onions, carrots, celery, fennel, leeks) diced
1 lb. fresh tomatoes, washed and coarsely chopped (or chopped canned with juice)
2 garlic cloves, finely minced
2 medium zucchini or summer squash or a combination, cut bite size
3 cups fresh greens shredded (spinach, chard, beet greens, kale)
½ cup fresh snap peas timed and halved or shelled peas
1 cup fresh string beans, trimmed and cut in 1-inch pieces
1 medium potato, diced
2 or 3 oz. Parmesan cheese
3 tbsp. olive oil
8 cups of water
1 whole skinned, boneless chicken breast cubed into bite size pieces
1 cup cooked white beans (or canned cannelloni work well)
An herb bouquet of your choice, tied up with kitchen string
Salt and pepper to taste

Warm the olive oil in the soup pot. Add the aromatic vegetables and soften slightly, about 5 minutes. Add garlic, tomatoes, water, Parmesan, herb bouquet, salt lightly (the cheese will add salt as it cooks), and bring to a simmer. Add potatoes and cook about 15 minutes. If you are using the chicken, add it in with the potatoes. Add string beans and cook another 10 minutes. Add zucchini, peas and greens and cook an additional 15 minutes. Taste for salt as you add each ingredient and add as necessary for your taste. Add beans and simmer 5 minutes more. If the soup is too thick for your taste, add water in small amounts. Fish out the herb bouquet and serve.

CHICKEN IN A CROCK POT

(Serves 4)

1 broiler cut up or chicken breast
1 – 10 oz. can low sodium cream of chicken soup
1 – 10 oz can low sodium cream of mushroom soup
1 cup mushroom pieces
1 bell pepper, sliced
1 onion, sliced
Dash salt, pepper and garlic powder
½ cup white wine
¼ tsp. Cajun spice such as Tony Chachere's
1 small butternut squash

Wash and dry chicken pieces. Place in crock pot. Mix remaining ingredients and pour over chicken. Cook on low for 6 to 7 hours or on high for 3 to 4 hours. Serve with noodles or rice.

WEST AFRICAN CHICKEN AND GROUNDNUT STEW

(Serves 8)

2 whole boneless, skinless chicken breasts cut into cubes
1 tbsp. peanut oil
1 medium onion, chopped
1 garlic clove, minced
1 – 28 oz. can low sodium diced tomatoes, un-drained
1 – 15 ½ oz. can great northern beans, un-drained
1 – 11 oz. can nibblets golden sweet corn, drained
1 sweet potato, peeled and chopped
¾ cup water
¼ cup peanut butter
1 tbsp. tomato paste
1 tsp. chili powder
½ tsp. ginger
½ tsp. cayenne
3 cups hot cooked rice

In a 4 quart Dutch oven over medium-high heat cook chicken in oil until chicken is lightly browned and no longer pink, stirring frequently. Add onion and garlic; cook and stir 3 to 4 minutes or until onion is tender. Add remaining ingredients except rice; mix well. Bring to a boil. Reduce heat to medium-low; cover and cook 30 minutes or until sweet potato is tender, stirring occasionally. If stew becomes too thick, add additional water. Serve stew over hot rice.

COCK 'N BULL STEW

(Serves 6 to 8)

¼ cup steak sauce
2 low sodium chicken bouillon cubes
½ tsp. pepper
1 tsp. sugar
½ cup hot water
1 lb. chicken breast, cut into 1 ½-inch cubes
1 lb. lean stewing beef, cut into 1 ½-inch cubes
1 medium onion, chopped
2 medium potatoes, peeled and cubed
2 medium carrots, diced
1 – 16 oz. can low sodium stewed tomatoes
¼ cup flour

Combine steak sauce, bouillon cubes, salt, pepper, sugar, and hot water in crock pot; stir well. Add remaining ingredients except flour; mix carefully. Cover and cook on low setting for 7 to 10 hours; on high setting for 4 hours. To thicken gravy, make a smooth paste of flour and ¼ cup of juices from stew. Stew into crock pot. Cover and cook on high setting until thickened.

FRENCH CHICKEN STEW

(Serves 6)

½ cup dry navy beans, soaked overnight and drained
2 cups water
4 – 6 chicken breasts, skinned, boned, and cubed
1 – 16 oz. can low sodium tomatoes
½ cup thinly sliced celery
½ cup diced carrot
½ cup chopped onion
1/8 tsp. garlic powder
1 bay leaf
½ tsp. crushed dry basil
1/8 tsp. powdered sage
¼ tsp. paprika
½ tsp. crushed, dried oregano
1 tsp. instant chicken bouillon (low sodium)
½ cup chicken broth (low sodium)

Place beans, 2 cups of water, and other ingredients in slow cooker/crock pot; cover and cook on low for 8 to 10 hours. Discard bay leaf before serving.

CREAM OF SWEET POTATO SOUP WITH CHICKEN

(Serves 6)

3 large sweet potatoes, peeled and sliced
2 cups low sodium chicken broth
1 tsp. sugar
1/8 tsp. ground cloves
1/8 tsp. nutmeg
Salt to taste
1 ½ cups half-and-half
1 lb chicken cut up into pieces

Put sweet potatoes, chicken, spices and broth in cooker. Cover and cook on high 4.5 hours or until potatoes are tender. Add half-and-half and cook ½ hour. Serve hot with a dollop of sour cream, if desired.

SEAFOOD

Joan and Anna
Ed and Ellie

SALMON CASSEROLE

(Serves 6)

2 eggs
1/2 c. cream
1 tsp. instant minced onion
1/8 tsp. pepper
½ tsp. basil
½ tsp. tarragon
1 can (12 oz.) whole kernel yellow corn, drained
2 cups frozen green beans
2 cans (7 3/4 oz.) salmon, drained & flaked or fresh baked salmon
3 oz. (3/4 c.) shredded Cheddar cheese
1 package mushrooms cut into small pieces
1 can tomato pieces (low salt or no salt added)

Mashed Potatoes (left-over's work great)

Heat oven to 350 degrees. In medium bowl beat eggs. Add remaining ingredients except cheese and mashed potatoes and mix well. Pour into a 1 1/2 quart casserole or small individual serving dishes. Top with mashed potatoes and sprinkle with cheese. Bake at 350 degrees for 45-50 minutes or until firm.

FISH CASSEROLE SUPREME

(Serves 6)

1 lb. of sole
1lb. Crabmeat
1/2 lb. crabmeat supreme
1/2 c. Ritz cracker crumbs
1/4 c. melted butter
1/4 tsp. salt (optional)
1/4 tsp.   White pepper (can use regular pepper, but the white makes it look prettier)
Thick White Sauce (see below)

Mix crabmeat, buttered crumbs, salt and pepper in a bowl. In a buttered casserole dish lay half of fish flat, place crabmeat mixture on top, then put remaining fish on top.

Pour white sauce over fish and bake in preheated oven at 350 degrees for 20 minutes or until fish flakes evenly.

THICK WHITE SAUCE:

3 or 4 tablespoons butter
3 tablespoons flour
1/4 teaspoon salt
1 cup milk or one half cup evaporated milk and 1/2 cup water

Melt butter in a sauce pan and whisk in flour and salt until smooth. Gradually stir in cold milk, cooking over direct heat and stirring constantly until sauce boils; reduce heat slightly and continue to stir until sauce becomes smooth and thick. When sauce thickens, simmer for an additional 10 minutes over very low heat, stirring occasionally.

Stir carefully to avoid lumps. If sauce becomes lumpy, use a stick blender or rotary beater to blend out lumps or else press through a sieve. Wondra flour may be used to great advantage since this flour does not have a tendency to lump.

FISH, RICE, AND TOMATO CASSEROLE

(Serves 4)

1 (16 oz.) can tomatoes (low salt or no salt added)
1 c. chicken broth (low sodium)
1/4 tsp. pepper
4 tbsp. butter, melted
1/2 lemon, thinly sliced
1 cup uncooked rice
1 lb. fresh or frozen sole or flounder
1/2 tsp. crushed basil
1/2 tsp. crushed tarragon

In a pan, mix tomatoes, chicken broth, pepper and 2 tablespoons butter. Stir in the rice. Cover and cook 20 minutes until rice is just tender.

Put rice in the bottom of a casserole dish or individual dishes and lay the thawed fillets over the rice and brush with the remaining butter. Sprinkle with tarragon and basil, if desired. Arrange the lemon slices, cut in halves, on fish. Bake uncovered for 15 minutes at 350 or until the fish flakes.

SO-O-O GOOD SALMON CASSEROLE

(Serves 4 to 6)

1 lb. salmon fillet (poached or baked), or 1 can salmon, drained
½ tsp. granulated garlic
1 tbsp. butter or oil of your choice
1 small onion, medium chop
½ red bell pepper, medium chop
1 cup frozen peas, thawed
2 celery ribs, medium chop
1 can corn
1 tsp. dried dill
1 tbsp. sherry, optional
½ cup mozzarella cheese, shredded
½ cup Cheddar cheese, shredded
7 slices wheat bread, toasted and torn into medium size pieces
5 eggs
1 cup cream, or half & half, or milk, or evaporated milk

Season the salmon and either poach in simmering water or bake on cookie sheet in 350 degrees oven until fish flakes easily with a fork (approximately 5 to 10 minutes depending on thickness of fillets). Once fish is done place it in separate bowl, pick for any bones, let cool and flake. Butter a 2 quart shallow casserole dish.

Heat a medium skillet, add butter, vegetables and dried dill. Sauté for 5 to 8 minutes. Add sherry and let reduce completely. Let vegetables cool down.

Place single layer of broken toast pieces in bottom of buttered casserole dish. Sprinkle with ½ of both cheeses. Top this with salmon, then vegetables, remaining cheese and top off with rest of toast pieces. In medium bowl make custard by beating eggs and cream. Season this mixture with salt and pepper and nutmeg. Pour egg custard over salmon casserole and let set in refrigerator for at least 2 hours and up to overnight. Bake in preheated 350 degree oven for 50 minutes or until a knife inserted in the center comes out clean. Let set 5 minutes before serving.

WAGON WHEEL SALMON PASTA

(Serves 6)

1 pound Radiatore, Wagon Wheels or other medium pasta shape, uncooked
1 pound salmon steaks, or one 14-oz. can salmon, drained
Freshly ground pepper
4 tbsp. chopped fresh dill
3 stalks celery, chopped (1 cup)
1 medium onion, chopped (1 cup)
1 carrot, sliced
2 tbsp. vegetable oil
2 tbsp. lemon juice
1 tbsp. white wine vinegar

Preheat oven to 350 degrees. Prepare pasta according to package directions; drain.

Place the salmon in a baking dish; season with pepper and dot with a little butter. Cover with aluminum foil and bake for 25 minutes. Remove the foil and cool. Remove the skin and bones; discard. Flake the salmon into large pieces and place in a large mixing bowl (If using canned salmon, place directly in the bowl and season with pepper). Add dill, celery, onion, carrot and pasta. In a small bowl, whisk together oil, lemon juice and vinegar. Add salmon and pasta and toss gently. Serve well chilled.

BAKED FISH WITH VEGGIES

(Serves 6)

6 (6-ounce) firm white fish fillets*
4 tablespoons butter, melted
2 clove large garlic, crushed
1 tablespoon dill weed
1/2 teaspoon ground black pepper
1 green pepper, seeded and cubed
1 orange or red pepper, seeded and cubed
1 medium onion, peeled and cubes
2 tomatoes, sliced in cubes
1 lemon, juiced
Cooked Rice or Noodles

*Use almost any firm, white-fleshed fish such as halibut, cod or bass.

Spray a shallow baking dish with vegetable cooking spray. Lay fish fillets in dish; skin side down. Mix butter, dill and garlic together and brush liberally over fish. Season with pepper. Layer peppers, onion and tomatoes over fish. Drizzle evenly with lemon juice.

Bake for 20 minutes at 350 degrees, or until fish flakes easily with a fork. Serve with rice or noodles.

Jerry's Parents - Kenneth and Doris June 2009

Baked Seafood Au Gratin

(Serves 8)

1 cup butter or margarine, divided use
1 cup all-purpose flour, divided use
1 pound crabmeat, picked over for shell and cartilage
4 cups water
1 pound medium shrimp, peeled and de-veined (no tails)
1/2 pound bay scallops
1/2 pound flounder fillets
3 cups milk
1 cup shredded sharp cheddar cheese
1 tablespoon white vinegar
1 teaspoon Worcestershire sauce
Pepper to taste
1 tsp. garlic, minced
1 tsp. Old Bay Seafood Seasoning
1/2 cup freshly grated Parmesan cheese

Lightly grease a 13 x 9 x 2-inch baking dish; or individual serving dishes and set aside.

In a large saucepan, put in 1/2 cup of the butter or margarine and stir in 1/2 cup of the flour and cook over medium heat for 5 minutes, stirring frequently. Add the crabmeat and mix well. Press this mixture into the bottom of the prepared baking dish and set aside.

In a large Dutch oven, bring the water to a boil. Add the shrimp, scallops and flounder. Simmer for 3 minutes. Drain, reserving 1 cup of the cooking liquid. Set the seafood aside.

In a large saucepan, melt the remaining 1/2 cup butter over low heat. Stir in the remaining 1/2 cup flour. Cook and stir constantly for 1 minute. Gradually add the milk plus the 1 cup reserved cooking liquid. Raise heat to medium and cook, stirring constantly, until the mixture is thickened and bubbly. Stir in the shredded cheddar cheese, vinegar, Worcestershire sauce, Old Bay, garlic and pepper, add the cooked seafood and stir gently.

Spoon the seafood mixture over the crabmeat crust and sprinkle with the Parmesan cheese. Bake at 350 degrees for 30 minutes or until lightly browned. Serve immediately.

Baked Tuna Noodle Casserole

(Serves 6)

1 (12-ounce) package egg noodles
1/4 cup butter
1 medium onion, chopped
2 stalks celery, chopped
1 small green bell pepper, chopped
1/4 cup all-purpose flour
2 1/2 cups milk
1 (12.5-ounce) can tuna (packed in water), drained
1 cup sliced mushrooms
1 teaspoon dried dill weed
½ teaspoon garlic powder
1/4 teaspoon ground pepper
2 cups cheddar cheese, grated
1/2 cup cracker or potato chip crumbs (use no salt if possible)

Grease 13 x 9 x 2-inch baking dish or individual baking dishes and set aside.

Cook noodles according to package directions.

Melt butter in medium-sized saucepan; add onion, celery, mushrooms and green pepper. Cook until vegetables have softened. Add flour and continue to cook, stirring constantly, for 1 minute. Slowly stir in milk; bring to a boil and cook for 2 minutes. Remove from heat. Add the tuna, dill weed, and pepper, gently stirring to mix.

Place half the cooked noodles in prepared baking dish. Spoon on half the tuna mixture and top with 1 cup cheese. Repeat with remaining half of ingredients in same order. Top with the crumbs. Bake at 350 degrees for 30 minutes or until golden and bubbly.

Salmon Quiche

(Serves 6)

2 tablespoons butter or margarine
1/2 cup chopped onion
1 clove garlic; minced
1 cup canned salmon, drained and flaked
1 (9-inch) unbaked pie crust
4 egg substitutes
1 cup low fat or skim milk
1 tablespoon all-purpose flour
1 teaspoon dried dill weed
1/4 teaspoon ground black pepper

Melt butter in a medium nonstick skillet over medium-high heat. Add onion and sauté until translucent, about 3 minutes. Add garlic sauté 1 more minute, or until pale golden. Add salmon and stir until heated. Spoon into prepared pie crust and set aside.

Whisk together the eggs substitute, milk, flour, dill, salt and pepper. Pour over salmon and bake for at 350 degrees 45 to 50 minutes or until knife inserted near center comes out clean. Let stand 10 minutes before serving.

Fish & Pasta Casserole

(Serves 6)

1 1/2 lb. fresh white fish fillets
1 3/4 cup skim or low fat milk
1 1/4 cup fish stock (Knorr's bouillon)
2 tablespoons butter
2 tablespoons flour
1 tablespoons chopped parsley
1 cup plain yogurt
2 eggs or egg substitute
1/2 lb cooked macaroni (use a small shape or noodles)
1 cup shredded cheddar cheese

Poach fish by placing fillets in a bubbling mixture of the milk and fish stock. The surface will just barely be moving, simmer for a few minutes. Turn off the heat and let the fish sit in the still-hot liquid for a few minutes longer until it's done. The poached fish is then ready Reserve 1 1/4 cup of the cooking liquid.

Melt butter in saucepan, add flour and stir for 2 min (DO NOT BROWN) add reserved cooking liquid and stir until thick. Add fish, parsley, and pepper to taste. Pour into 2
Quart casserole dish. In a separate bowl, combine yogurt, eggs, 1/3 cup shredded cheese
& macaroni. Mix well. Pour over fish mixture. Sprinkle with remaining cheese. Bake
about 30 min. at 375 degrees.

EASY FISH CASSEROLE

(Serves 6-8)

1 package halibut or other white fish
1 teaspoon Dill weed
½ teaspoon garlic powder
1 tablespoon butter
8 oz. egg noodles
10 oz. mixed vegetables
½ cup half-and-half
½ cup milk
1 can low sodium cream of mushroom soup
1 cup low fat or no fat sour cream
2 teaspoons Worcestershire sauce
½ teaspoon onion powder

Place fish on a tin foil covered cookie sheet or other baking sheet. Sprinkle garlic powder, dill weed and top with butter. Bake for 15 minutes or until fish flakes apart; set aside.

Cook noodles and vegetables according to directions on each package. Drain noodles and vegetables; add to casserole dish stir to combine.

Combine remaining ingredients in a shallow 2-quart casserole dish and place fish on top; bake uncovered at 350 degrees for 10 minutes.

COD AND POTATO CASSEROLE

(Serves 6)

2 pounds cod fish
2 cups skim milk
5 large potatoes, peeled and sliced
1 large onion, sliced
3/4 cup olive oil
2 cloves garlic, minced
1 tablespoon chopped fresh parsley
1 teaspoon paprika
1 tablespoon Italian seasoning
3 tablespoons tomato sauce
1 cup cheddar cheese

Poach fish by placing fillets in slow simmering milk. The surface will just barely be moving, simmer for a few minutes. Turn off the heat and let the fish sit in the still-hot liquid for a few minutes longer until it's done.

In an 8x11 casserole dish, layer half the potato slices, all of the cod, and all of the onions. Top with remaining potato slices. In a small bowl, mix together olive oil, garlic, parsley, Italian seasoning, paprika, and tomato sauce. Pour evenly over casserole. Top with cheddar cheese. Bake casserole at 375 degrees for 45 minutes or until potatoes are soft and tender.

Ellie, Tom, Ed, Joan, Mary
Matt and Aaron

TURKEY SAUSAGE AND TORTELLINI SOUP

(Serves 6)

12 oz. turkey sausage
12 oz. Sweet Italian sausage
1 cup loose-pack frozen cut green beans or Italian-style green beans
3 – 14 ½ oz. cans Italian-style stewed tomatoes
3 cups turkey stock or low sodium chicken broth
1 medium zucchini squash – cubed
1 medium yellow squash – cubed
2 medium carrots – shredded
2 ribs celery - cubed
1 package of dry onion soup mix (can be full of salt leave out if on salt restricted diet)
2 - 9 oz. packages of refrigerated cheese filled tortellini
Parmesan cheese – freshly grated if possible

Brown turkey sausage and sweet Italian sausage and drain off fat. Place in crock pot.
Add package of onion soup mix and the chicken broth to the crock pot. Stir.
Add green beans, squash, carrots, celery and the cans of un-drained tomatoes to the pot.
Cook 4 hours on high. Stir in the tortellini cover and cook 30 min to 1 hour. Ladle soup into bowls and sprinkle with Parmesan cheese.

If you use the dried tortellini, add with all the rest of the ingredients and cook 5 to 6 hours on high.

TURKEY TETRAZZINE

(Serves 6)

8 oz. (about 4 cups) wide or extra wide egg noodles, uncooked
Vegetable cooking spray
2 cups low-sodium chicken broth
2 cups diced, boneless, skinless, cooked turkey
12 oz. mushrooms, thinly sliced
1 small onion, peeled and thinly sliced
¼ cup chopped fresh parsley
1 bay leaf
1 cup milk
2 tbsp. cornstarch
4 tbsp. dry bread crumbs
1 tsp. olive or vegetable oil
2 tbsp. grated Parmesan cheese

Cook pasta according to package directions. While pasta is cooking, lightly spray an 11x7 inch baking dish with vegetable spray. Combine chicken broth, turkey, mushrooms, onion, parsley and bay leaf in a 2 quart saucepan over medium heat. Heat to boiling, cover pot and cook 5 minutes.

Stir milk and cornstarch together in a small bowl until cornstarch is dissolved. Stir milk mixture into the saucepan. Heat to boiling, stirring constantly. Reduce heat to simmering. Simmer covered for 3 minutes.

When pasta is done, drain well and return to pot. Remove bay leaf from sauce and pour sauce into pot. Stir until pasta is coated with sauce. Transfer mixture to the prepared baking dish.

Mix the bread crumbs, oil and parmesan cheese together in a small bowl until evenly blended. Sprinkle mixture over pasta. Bake at 350 degrees until crumbs are golden brown and edges are bubbling, about 20 minutes. Serve hot.

MEDITERRANEAN TURKEY CASSEROLE

(Serves 8)

1 lb. medium egg noodles, uncooked
1 – 14 ½ oz. can low-sodium chicken broth
1 cup skim milk
1 tsp. salt
¼ cup cornstarch
2 cups chopped cooked turkey
1 – 14 oz. can artichoke hearts, drained and quartered
1 – 7 ½ oz. jar roasted red peppers, drained and sliced
9 Kalamata olives, pitted and sliced
½ cup grated part-skim mozzarella cheese
½ cup white wine
1 tsp. fresh lemon juice
½ tsp. black pepper
¼ tsp. garlic powder
½ tsp. Italian spices
Vegetable oil cooking spray
2 tbsp. grated Parmesan cheese

Prepare noodles according to package directions; drain. Stir the broth, milk, salt and cornstarch together in a large pot or Dutch oven until the cornstarch is dissolved. Cook over medium heat, stirring constantly, until thickened and bubbly. Stir in noodles, turkey, artichoke hearts, red peppers, olives, mozzarella cheese, wine, lemon juice and spices.

Spray a 3 quart baking dish with cooking spray. Spoon into baking dish. Sprinkle with Parmesan cheese. Bake until bubbling around the edges, about 35 minutes at 350 degrees. Let stand 5 minutes before serving.

TURKEY, BROCCOLI, AND SWEET POTATO CASSEROLE

(Serves 4)

1 ½ cups diced cooked sweet potato
2 cups diced cook turkey meat
1 ½ cups broccoli, carrots, and snow peas
2 cups giblet gravy
2 oz. almonds, toasted and slivered

In a pan-sprayed, 8" or 9" square casserole dish, place the potatoes on the bottom. Next layer is the turkey meat. Next layer is the vegetable medley. Then pour on the gravy, allowing it to sink to the bottom and thus moisturize all of the ingredients. Finally, sprinkle on the nuts. Place on the middle shelf of the preheated 350 degree oven uncovered for 45 minutes, or until the edges are browned and bubbly. Serve hot.

TURKEY AND SWEET POTATO CASSEROLE

(Serves 4)

3 medium (6 ¼ - 6 ½ oz. each) sweet potatoes, peeled and cut into 2" pieces
1 - 10 oz. pkg. frozen cut green beans
1 ½ lb. turkey cutlets
1 – 12 oz. jar home-style turkey gravy
2 tbsp. flour
¼ tsp. Cajun spice mix such as Tony's Chachere's
1 tsp. parsley flakes
¼ - ½ tsp. dried rosemary leaves, crumbled
1/8 tsp. pepper

Layer sweet potatoes, green beans, and turkey in slow cooker. Combine remaining ingredients until smooth. Pour over mixture in slow cooker. Cover. Cook on low 8 to 10 hours.
Serve with biscuits and cranberry sauce.

SUPPER-TIME STEW

16oz. ground 90% lean turkey or beef
1 cup (15 oz) sliced raw potatoes
1 ½ cups chopped celery
2 cups sliced carrots
1 cup chopped onion
1 ½ cups frozen peas
1 ½ cups frozen green beans
1 ¾ cups (15 oz. can) low sodium tomato sauce
2 tsp. Italian seasoning

In a large skillet sprayed with butter-flavored cooking spray, brown meat. Meanwhile, in a slow cooker, combine potatoes, celery, carrots, onion, and peas. Spoon browned meat over vegetables. In a small bowl, combine tomato sauce and Italian seasoning. Evenly pour sauce over meat. Cover and cook on Low for 6 to 8 hours. Mix well before serving. Serve with cornbread if desired.

TURKEY AND SWEET-POTATO SOUP

(Serves 4)

2 tbsp. butter
1 onion, curt into thin slices
1 ½ teaspoons dried sage
1 lb. sweet potatoes, peeled and cut into ½-inch cubes
1 ½ quarts canned low-sodium chicken broth or homemade stock
¼ lb. green beans cut into ¼-inch pieces
¼ tsp. fresh-ground black pepper
1 lb. turkey cutlets cut into cubes (or ground turkey)

In a large pot, melt the butter over moderately low heat. Add the onion and sage and cook, stirring occasionally, until the onion is translucent, about 5 minutes.

Add the sweet potatoes and broth. Bring to a boil. Reduce the heat and simmer until the sweet potatoes are tender, about 10 minutes.

Transfer half the soup to the food processor or blender and puree. Return the pureed soup to the pot and add the green beans, and the pepper. Simmer until the beans are just tender, about 8 minutes.

Stir in the turkey. Cook until the turkey is just done, about 1 ½ minutes.

Turkey Options:
If you like, you may use ground turkey or ground turkey sausage. The sweet Italian sausage works great. Brown the ground turkey before adding to the simmering beans.

TURKEY COBBLER

(Serves 6)

4 tablespoons butter
2 ribs celery, sliced
1 bunch green onions, about 6 to 8, thinly sliced
6 tablespoons flour
2 cups low sodium chicken broth
1 cup leftover or canned turkey gravy, or use more chicken broth
1/8 teaspoon freshly ground black pepper
1/4 teaspoon poultry seasoning
2 cups frozen mixed vegetables, thawed
3 cups diced leftover cooked turkey

Topping:
2 packages of cornbread mix brand of your choice.

Or follow recipe below:
1 large egg
1/2 milk
4 tablespoons melted butter
1 cup all-purpose flour
1 cup cornmeal
2 teaspoons baking powder
1 tablespoon granulated sugar, optional
1/4 teaspoon salt
1 scant teaspoon poultry seasoning or crumbled rubbed sage
1 teaspoon dried parsley flakes, optional

In a large saucepan, heat 4 tablespoons butter over medium-low heat until frothy; add celery and cook until celery is tender. Add green onions and cook 1 minute longer. Add 6 tablespoons flour, stirring until well blended and bubbly.

Add chicken broth and turkey gravy; continue cooking, stirring, until thickened and bubbly. Add seasonings, thawed vegetables, and turkey; heat through. Pour into a buttered 9-inch square pan or 2-quart baking dish.

Topping: Prepare according to package directions. With a wooden spoon, stir dry ingredients into the egg and milk mixture. Add poultry seasoning and dried parsley until well blended. Drop spoonfuls of the dough all over the hot filling. Bake for 30 to 35 minutes at 400 degrees or until topping is browned and filling is bubbly. Serve with cranberry sauce on the side, if desired.

Ellie and Eddie on their 50th Anniversary

ALMOND AND TURKEY NOODLE CASSEROLE

(Serves 6)

4 tablespoons butter
1/4 cup all-purpose flour
2 cups low fat milk
Pepper, to taste
2 tablespoons dry white wine or sherry, optional
2 egg substitutes
3 cups turkey, cooked, diced
1 cup frozen English peas, thawed
1/4 cup slivered almonds
3 tablespoons Italian bread crumbs
1 tablespoon butter
2 tablespoons Parmesan cheese, grated
12 oz. cooked noodles of your choice

Prepare noodles according to package and set aside.

In a 2-quart saucepan over medium-low heat, melt butter; add flour and stir until smooth and bubbly. Gradually add milk, stirring constantly, until sauce is thickened and smooth. Add pepper, and wine or sherry, if used.

In a medium bowl, pour in egg substitutes add a little of the hot sauce to the eggs. Stirring constantly, add the egg mixture back into the hot sauce mixture. Stir in turkey, peas, noodles and half of the slivered almonds. Pour into a 2-quart baking dish. Sprinkle with remaining almonds and crumbs; dot with butter and sprinkle with cheese. Brown under the broiler until cheese is melted.

MEXICAN TURKEY SHELLS

(Serves 8)

1 lb ground turkey or Italian sweet sausage (removed from casing)
1 can spinach, drained
1 tsp minced garlic
1 tsp oregano
½ tsp cumin
1 cup ricotta cheese
18 large pasta shells, uncooked
1 can (20 oz) enchilada sauce
1 cup Monterrey Jack cheese, shredded

In large bowl combine turkey, spinach, garlic, oregano, and cumin. Blend in ricotta. Stuff each uncooked shell with turkey mixture. Pour half the enchilada sauce in bottom of large glass baking dish. Arrange stuffed shells in dish and dot with any remaining turkey mixture. Pour remaining enchilada sauce over shells and cover tightly with foil. Bake in a pre-heated 375°F oven for 75 minutes or until shells are tender. Sprinkle cheese over top, recover, and allow to stand 10 minutes before serving.

TURKEY AND BROCCOLI CASSEROLE

(Serves 6)

2 cups (4 ounces) medium-wide noodles
1 package frozen broccoli pieces
3 tablespoons butter or margarine
3 tablespoons flour
1/4 teaspoon prepared mustard
1/4 teaspoon pepper
2 cups milk
1 cup (1/4 lb.) grated processed American cheese
2 cups cubed left over turkey
1/3 cup slivered, toasted almonds

Cook noodles in boiling water until tender; drain.

Cook broccoli as label directs until just tender; drain.

In saucepan over low heat melt butter; stir in flour, salt, mustard, pepper and milk. Cook, stirring constantly, until thick and smooth. Remove from heat and stir in cheese until melted.

In greased shallow casserole or 8-inch-square baking dish, arrange noodles, broccoli and turkey; pour cheese sauce over all and sprinkle with almonds. Bake uncovered at 350 degrees F. for 15 minutes, or until bubbling hot.

Creamy Creole Turkey Bake

(Serves 4)

2/3 cup chopped onion
2/3 cup chopped celery
1/3 cup chopped green pepper
1 garlic clove, minced, or 1/4 teaspoon garlic powder
1 tablespoon margarine
1/4 pound mushrooms, sliced
8 ounces cream cheese, softened
1 can (8 ounces) low sodium stewed and diced tomatoes, drained
1 1/2 teaspoons Cajun seasoning such as Tony Chachere
8 ounces spiral, cooked according to package directions
3 cups 1/2-inch cubed cooked turkey
vegetable cooking spray
1/2 cup grated Parmesan cheese

In medium non-stick skillet, over medium-high heat, sauté onion, celery, green pepper and garlic in margarine 4 to 5 minutes or until vegetables are crisp-tender. Add mushrooms and sauté 2 minutes. Remove from heat.

In medium bowl blend cream cheese, tomatoes and Cajun seasoning. Fold in vegetable mixture, cooked noodles and turkey. Pour mixture into 9-inch square dish, sprayed with vegetable cooking spray. Sprinkle cheese over top and bake at 325 degrees F. 30 minutes or until bubbly.

Mary Liz and Joan

SAUSAGE CASSEROLE WITH POTATOES

(Serves 4)

4 cups sliced potatoes
2 medium carrots, sliced
1 cup frozen green beans, thawed
1 white onion
2 tbsp. butter
2 tbsp. flour
1 ½ cups low sodium beef broth
¼ teaspoon pepper
1 lb. pork or turkey sausage
Chopped fresh parsley, optional

Cook potatoes and carrots in boiling salted water just until tender; drain. Place in a lightly buttered casserole Sauté onions until they are clear in color and add to potatoes and carrots in casserole dish. Melt butter in a saucepan over low heat; stir in flour. Gradually add beef broth, stirring constantly. Cook and stir until thickened.

Add pepper to sauce; pour over vegetables in casserole. Sauté the port or turkey sausage slowly until just cooked through. Drain the fat out of the sausage and place on top of potato mixture in casserole. Cover with lid or foil and bake at 375 degrees for 20 minutes, or until the vegetables are tender and casserole is hot. Sprinkle with chopped fresh parsley before serving.

PARTY HAM CASSEROLE

4 oz. noodles
1 – 10 ¾ oz. can condensed low sodium cream of mushroom soup
½ cup milk
1 tsp. instant minced onion
1 tsp. prepared mustard
1 cup sour cream
2 cups cooked ham, cut in 1-inch pieces
1 cup frozen green beans, thawed
1 tbsp. grated Parmesan cheese

To de-salt the ham, place ham into a pot containing enough water to cover the ham. Bring to a boil and simmer for 15 minutes. Strain water out of pot and add new water to cover the ham. Bring to a boil and simmer for 15 minutes. Strain water out of pot. The ham now has much less salt.

Cook noodles as directed on package; drain.

While noodles are cooking, combine in a small saucepan the soup and milk, stirring over low heat until smooth. Add onion, mustard and sour cream. In a greased 1 ½ quart casserole dish, layer half of the noodles, half of the ham and sauce. Repeat layers. Top with grated cheese. Bake uncovered at 325 degrees for 25 minutes, or until golden brown and bubbly.

SLOW COOKER KIELBASA STEW

(Serves 8)

2 lb. kielbasa sausage, cut into 1-inch pieces
1 ½ lb. sauerkraut, drained and rinsed
2 Granny Smith apples, peeled, cored, and chopped
¾ onion, chopped
2 lb. red potatoes, chopped
1 ½ cup low sodium chicken broth
½ tsp. caraway seeds
½ cup shredded Swiss cheese

Place half the sausage in a slow cooker, and top with the sauerkraut. Cover with the remaining sausage, apples, and onion. Top with the potatoes. Pour chicken broth over all, and sprinkle with caraway seeds.

Cover and cook on high for 4 hour, or until potatoes are tender. Top each serving with Swiss cheese.

PORK AND CHICKEN ADOBO

(Serves 4)

1 ¼ lb. boneless pork loin roast, cut into 2-inch pieces
1 ¼ pounds boneless, skinless chicken breast, cut into 2-inch pieces
3 tbsp. salt
1 tbsp. black peppercorns, coarsely ground
2 tbsp. crushed garlic
2 bay leaves
1 cup white vinegar
¼ cup low sodium soy sauce (optional)
1 tbsp. olive oil
2 cloves garlic, minced
Cooked rice

Season pork and chicken with salt and pepper and place in a stock pot. Rub with crushed garlic and bay leaf, and coat with vinegar (and soy sauce, if using). Cover and marinate in the refrigerator for 8 hours or overnight.

Bring meat and marinating liquid to a boil. Reduce to a simmer and cook for 1 ½ hours, or until meat is fork-tender. If necessary, add a small amount of water to prevent drying out.

Strain liquid from meat. Return to the stock pot and bring to a simmer. In a skillet, cook and stir meat in 1 tablespoon of oil over medium –high heat until brown on all sides, adding remaining 2 cloves of minced garlic in the last 3 minutes. Add meats to cooking liquid, and continue simmering until slightly thickened. Serve hot over cooked rice.

SAUSAGE, BEANS AND BROCCOLI RABE STEW

(Serves 4)

1 tbsp. extra-virgin olive oil
1 ¼ lb. Italian bulk sweet sausage
1 medium onion, chopped
1 carrot, chopped
1 large potato, peeled and chopped
2 cloves garlic, minced
1 bay leaf
2 cans white beans, drained
Pepper to taste
4 cups chopped broccoli rabe
1 quart low sodium chicken stock
Grated Parmesan cheese

Heat medium soup pot over medium-high heat. Add the olive oil and sausage and brown. Discard fat from pad. Add veggies, bay leaf, and beans. Season with pepper. Cook mixture 5 minutes to begin to soften the vegetables. Add washed rabe and stock and cover pot. Bring soup to a boil. Reduce heat to simmer and cook 15 minutes. Adjust seasonings and serve soup with grated cheese, for topping.

HAM AND LENTIL STEW

(Serves 6)

2 cups lentils
½ lb. ham, diced
1 onion, chopped
1 bay leaf
2 ribs celery, chopped
1 clove garlic, minced
Pepper to taste

Combine all ingredients with 2 quarts water in the crock pot. Cook on low covered for 8 to 10 hours. Adjust seasonings and serve.

MULLIGATAWNY

(Serves 6)

1 ½ lb. lamb stew meat, diced (you may substitute pork meat)
4 tbsp. butter
1 onion, minced
1 tbsp. curry powder
2 tbsp. flour
1/3 cup lentils
2 tart apples, peeled and diced
1 bell pepper, diced
2 carrots, diced
1 tsp. sugar
½ tsp. ground mace
¼ tsp. ground cloves
Pepper to taste
1 cup coconut milk

Brown the meat in butter in a skillet. Add onion, curry powder, and flour and cook and stir for 2 minutes. Combine with remaining ingredients, except coconut milk, and 2 quarts of water in the crock pot. Cover and cook on low 8 to 10 hours. Add coconut milk, heat through, and serve with rice.

AUNT RITA'S PIGEONS

(Serves 5)

Cut the core out of a small to medium sized cabbage and steam leaves for a few minutes with the core-side down. You want the leaves soft so you can roll them, but not fully cooked.

3 lbs of raw ground pork (or ½ & ½ pork and beef)
1/3 to ½ cup cooked rice
Onion
2 cloves garlic
Butter
Tomato soup

Sauté onion and garlic in butter till onions are clear.
Add onion/garlic mixture to the rice and meat.

Place meat in the steamed cabbage leaves and roll.

You may freeze them after they are rolled, but do not freeze after cooking.

When ready to cook place pigeons in baking dish with some water. Steam pigeons for a few minutes and add canned tomato soup and serve.

Makes 20 or more pigeons.

Aunt Rita, Aunt Stella, Ellie (the tall one), Helen Louise

LIVER AND PORK MEATLOAF

1 lb. liver, slices
3/4 c. boiling water
1 med. onion
1/2 lb. pork sausage meat
1 c. dry bread crumbs
1 tbsp. Worcestershire sauce
1 tbsp. lemon juice
1/8 tsp. pepper
2 eggs
4 slices bacon

Pour the boiling water over the liver and simmer 5 minutes. Remove the liver and grind with the onions through the meat knife of a food chopper. Add to the stock with the remaining ingredients except bacon. Place in loaf pan, top with bacon and bake for 45 minutes at 350 degrees.

PORK AND PASTA

(Serves 6)

3/4 lb. rigatoni
1 lb. ground pork
16 oz. ricotta cheese
1/2 c. parsley, chopped
2 tbsp. grated Parmesan cheese
1/2 tsp. basil
1 (32 oz.) jar spaghetti sauce
16 oz. Mozzarella cheese

Start water for macaroni, brown pork. Cook and drain macaroni. Drain off excess fat from pork. Add ricotta cheese to pork, mix. Add next three ingredients and half the sauce. Mix thoroughly with macaroni. Pour into 13 x 9 inch pan. Add remaining sauce, cover top of pasta. Sprinkle Mozzarella cheese over pasta and sauce. Cook at 350 degrees for half an hour. Enjoy!

Serve with salad and garlic bread.

Sausage and Apple Casserole

(Serves 6-8)

1 1/2 lbs. bulk sausage rolled in small balls
1 tablespoon flour
2 teaspoons sugar
¼ teaspoon nutmeg
1 teaspoon cinnamon
4 medium apples peeled and cut into pieces
3 medium sweet potatoes cut into pieces

Fry sausage balls, save drippings. Combine flour, nutmeg, cinnamon, and sugar. Arrange sausage, apples and potatoes in layers in a casserole dish. Sprinkle a little of the flour mix over each layer. Top with a layer of sausage. Sprinkle casserole with 1 tablespoon of the sausage drippings. Cover tightly. Bake at 375degrees for 1 hour.

HAM AND POTATO CASSEROLE

(Serves 6)

2 lbs. frozen hash brown potatoes, thawed
1 can low sodium cream of chicken soup
½ cup melted butter
16 oz. no-fat sour cream
2 c. cubed ham, de-salted
½ tsp. pepper
1 ½ c. shredded Cheddar cheese
¼ c. butter, melted

To de-salt the ham, place ham into a pot containing enough water to cover the ham. Bring to a boil and simmer for 15 minutes. Strain water out of pot and add new water to cover the ham. Bring to a boil and simmer for 15 minutes. Strain water out of pot. The ham now has much less salt.

Combine all casserole ingredients and mix well. Place in casserole dish. Combine topping ingredients; sprinkle on casserole. Bake at 350 degrees for 1 hour.

Ellie a few months before she passed

TORTELLINI BAKE

(Serves 4)

1 teaspoon butter
2 pounds Tortellini (meat or cheese) cooked according to package
1 cup Parmigiano-Reggiano or Parmesan cheese
1 jar Alfredo sauce

Put cooked tortellini in the bottom of a baking dish or individual serving dish. Spoon Alfredo sauce over the pasta. Sprinkle the cheese over the sauce. Place in the oven and bake for about 8 to 10 minutes or until the cheese is golden and bubbly.

CHICKEN LASAGNA

(Serves 12)

9 lasagna noodles
1/2 cup butter
1 onion, chopped
1 clove garlic, minced
1/2 cup all-purpose flour
2 cups low sodium chicken broth
1 1/2 cups milk
4 cups shredded mozzarella cheese, divided
1 cup grated Parmesan cheese, divided
1 teaspoon dried basil
1 teaspoon dried oregano
1/2 teaspoon ground black pepper
2 cups ricotta cheese
2 cups cubed, cooked chicken meat
2 (10 ounce) packages frozen chopped spinach, thawed and drained
1 tablespoon chopped fresh parsley
1/4 cup grated Parmesan cheese for topping

Bring a large pot of lightly salted water to a boil. Cook lasagna noodles in boiling water for 8 to 10 minutes. Drain, and rinse with cold water.

Melt the butter in a large saucepan over medium heat. Cook the onion and garlic in the butter until tender, stirring frequently. Stir in the flour and simmer until bubbly. Mix in the broth and milk, and boil, stirring constantly, for 1 minute. Stir in 2 cups mozzarella cheese and 1/2 cup Parmesan cheese. Season with the basil, oregano, and ground black pepper. Remove from heat, and set aside.

Spread 1/3 of the sauce mixture in the bottom of a 9x13 inch baking dish. Layer with 1/3 of the noodles, the ricotta, and the chicken. Arrange 1/3 of the noodles over the chicken, and layer with 1/3 of the sauce mixture, spinach, and the remaining 2 cups mozzarella cheese and 1/2 cup Parmesan cheese. Arrange remaining noodles over cheese, and spread remaining sauce evenly over noodles. Sprinkle with parsley and 1/4 cup Parmesan cheese.
Bake 40 minutes at 350 degrees.

TRADITIONAL LASAGNA

(Serves 8)

2 lbs. lean ground beef
1/2 lb dry lasagna noodles (requires 9 lasagna noodles - unbroken)
1 teaspoon sugar
1 28 oz can low sodium tomato sauce
1/2 28 oz can (16 oz) low sodium stewed tomatoes, diced
1/2 6 oz can (3 oz) Italian tomato paste
1 lb low fat Ricotta cheese
1 1/2 lb Mozzarella cheese, shredded
3/4 lb freshly grated parmesan cheese
Garlic Power
Oregano
Italian Spice
Parsley diced (fresh flat leaf preferred)
1 Garlic Cloves, minced
1 cup red wine or 1-12 oz. beer (any kind)

Brown lean ground beef in skillet until lightly browned and cooked through. Drain off and dispose of excess beef fat. Add tomato sauce, tomato paste, tomatoes, oregano, parsley, garlic, Italian Spice Mix to taste, probably 2 teaspoons of each. Add red wine or beer and a teaspoon of sugar. Stir and allow sauce to simmer 15-45 minutes to thicken. If it becomes too thick, just add a bit of water to thin.

Cook 1 lb lasagna noodles in a large pot per cooking directions. Add a dash of olive oil and salt to prevent the noodles from sticking together. Drain in colander and place in cool water filled pan to keep from drying out and sticking together.

In 9 x 13 pan, ladle one cup of sauce and spread along the bottom of the pan. Apply a layer noodles 3 length wise (edges overlapping). Ladle in sauce sparingly into center trough of 3 noodles. Apply a layer of mozzarella cheese slices on top of lasagna sauce. Place ricotta cheese dollops (about a Tablespoon) every 2 inches in center of noodles on top of mozzarella cheese slices, sprinkle grated parmesan cheese in thin even layer on top of ricotta cheese. Apply second layer of noodles, repeat three times stopping with noodles. If you have extra sauce and cheese you can spread that over the top. Bake at 375°F for 45 minutes. Allow to sit 15 minutes before serving.

EGGPLANT LASAGNE

(Serves 8)

2 teaspoons vegetable oil
3 cups eggplant, unpeeled & diced
3/4 cup chopped onion
1 teaspoon garlic, minced
28 ounces low sodium tomatoes, canned and diced
1/2 teaspoon sugar
1/4 teaspoon basil
1 pound carrots, shredded
10 ounces spinach, drained
15 ounces ricotta cheese, part skim milk
1 cup mozzarella cheese, part skim milk, shredded
1 large egg, beaten
1 pinch nutmeg
9 lasagna noodles, cooked
2 tablespoons grated Parmesan cheese, fresh

Cook lasagna noodles according to package add a dash of olive oil to the water before adding noodles. Drain and place in cool water.

Eggplant sauce, in large nonstick skillet, heat oil over medium-high heat. Add eggplant, onions and garlic; cook, stirring, 5 minutes. Stir in tomatoes, sugar, and basil. Bring to boil; reduce heat to low, cover and simmer until eggplant is tender, 20 minutes.

Bring 2 quarts water to boil in large saucepan. Add carrots and cook 1 minute; drain. Combine carrots, spinach, ricotta, mozzarella, egg, and the nutmeg in large bowl. Spoon 1-1/4 cups eggplant sauce in 9 x 13-inch baking dish.

Layer with 3 lasagna noodles and half the spinach mixture, 3 more noodles and 1-3/4 cups sauce, then remaining spinach and noodles. Top with remaining sauce. Sprinkle with Parmesan. Bake uncovered in a 357 degree oven 30 to 40 minutes, until hot.

STUFFED SHELLS WITH BROCCOLI

(Serves 8-10)

24 Jumbo Shells, uncooked
1 10-oz. package frozen chopped broccoli, thawed
1 cup part-skim ricotta cheese
1/2 cup shredded Swiss cheese
2 14 1/2-oz. cans diced low sodium tomatoes
1/2 tsp. dried basil
1/2 tsp. dried oregano
Salt and freshly ground black pepper to taste

Prepare pasta according to package directions; drain. Combine broccoli, ricotta cheese, Swiss cheese, oregano, basil, salt and pepper. Stir together until well blended. Pour about 1 cup tomatoes over bottom of 13 x 9 x 2-inch baking pan, breaking up tomatoes with a fork. Spoon 1 round tablespoon of cheese mixture into each shell and place open-side up in an even layer in the pan. Pour remaining tomatoes over and around shells. Cover pan with foil. Bake at 375 degrees for 25 minutes until heated through, and serve.

BAKED MANICOTTI

(Serves 6)

8 oz. Manicotti, uncooked
1 15-oz. container part-skim ricotta cheese, whipped until smooth
1/2 cup grated Parmesan cheese
1 egg, beaten
1 cup canned spinach
2 tsp. parsley flakes
1/4 tsp. pepper
1 26-oz. jar spaghetti sauce
Grated Parmesan cheese for topping

Prepare pasta according to package directions; drain. In medium bowl, blend ricotta, Parmesan, egg and spinach. Stir in parsley and pepper. Stuff pasta with cheese mixture and arrange in a 13 x 9-inch baking dish. Pour spaghetti sauce evenly over pasta. Sprinkle with additional Parmesan cheese. Cover. Bake pasta in a 350 degree oven until hot approximately 35 minutes.

Eddie and Rayme (Dad's Nephew)

EGGPLANT CASSEROLE

(Serves 6)

8 oz. Medium Egg Noodles, uncooked
1 eggplant, peeled and cut into 1/4-inch slices
1/2 cup egg substitute
3/4 cup fine dry bread crumbs
1 16-oz. can low-sodium tomato sauce
1/2 tsp. garlic powder
1/8 tsp. pepper
1/2 tsp. oregano
1/3 cup grated Parmesan cheese, divided
4 oz. part-skim mozzarella cheese, thinly sliced, divided

Prepare noodles according to package directions. While noodles are cooking, dip each slice of eggplant into egg substitute, then into bread crumbs. Coat each side well. Spray a cookie sheet with vegetable cooking spray. Place eggplant slices on cookie sheet and place under broiler for 3 to 4 minutes on each side, or until lightly browned.

Preheat oven to 375 degrees. In a medium bowl, combine tomato sauce, garlic powder, pepper and oregano.

When noodles are done, drain well. Spray a 2-quart baking dish with cooking spray. Place a layer of eggplant in bottom of baking dish. Layer half the noodles, followed by half the tomato mixture. Sprinkle half the Parmesan cheese and half the mozzarella cheese on top. Cover with foil and bake for 30 minutes. Remove foil and continue baking 15 minutes, until cheese is melted and top is lightly browned.

BAKED ZITI

(Serves 6)

1-16 oz box of ziti, bow ties or rigatoni
1 ½ lb ground beef
1 lb. cheddar cheese, grated
2 large cans diced low sodium tomatoes
1 ¼ cups grated Parmesan cheese
1 teaspoon Italian seasoning
¼ teaspoon pepper
pinch of red pepper flakes (optional)

In a large pot, boil the pasta in water until still slightly firm (al-dente). Pasta will cook a little more while baking. When the pasta is cooked, drain well and place in a greased casserole pan or baking dish.

Brown the ground beef in a sauté pan. Remove fat from pan. Add pepper, Italian seasonings and tomatoes. Add the browned beef and tomatoes to the noodles; mix gently. Sprinkle 2/3 of the sharp cheddar and gently mix in.

Top the pasta with a blend of the Parmesan and cheddar, sprinkling evenly over the top.

Place in a preheated 350°F degree oven and bake for 40 to 50 minutes until the top is lightly brown and the sauce and cheese is bubbly.

WHITE OR RED BAKED RAVIOLI

(Serves 6)

1 box frozen meat or cheese ravioli (48 to 50 to box)
1 qt. spaghetti sauce (RED) or 2 jars of Alfredo or garlic herb sauce (WHITE)
16 oz. Mozzarella cheese, shredded
1 (24 oz.) container cottage cheese
1 can drained spinach (optional)
4 egg substitutes

Spray baking dish with non-stick vegetable spray. Pour a cup of the sauce on the bottom of the dish and place a layer of ravioli. In a bowl combine the 4 egg substitutes, drained spinach with the cottage cheese. Mix together and put half of mixture over ravioli. Pour sauce over the cheese mix. Cover with half of Mozzarella cheese and egg mixture. Top with remaining Mozzarella cheese. Bake at 325 degrees for 1 hour.

BEEF AND CHESSE BAKE

(Serves 6-8)
1 15 oz. can of low sodium tomato sauce
1 clove minced garlic
1 teaspoon Italian seasoning
5 ounces of cream cheese, light or fat free
8 ounces of sour cream, light or fat free
¼ cup cottage cheese, light or fat free
1 box of bow tie pasta
1 package of lean ground beef
2 teaspoons of Herbs de Provence
¼ cup Parmesan cheese

Boil pasta according to package directions. Drain pasta, and add to greased baking dish
Brown ground beef in pan. Drain fat from pan. Add herbs de province to ground beef. Add tomato sauce, garlic, and Italian seasoning to ground beef and simmer on low.

Combine sour cream, cream cheese, cottage cheese and green onions. Spread cheese mixture over pasta. And pour beef mixture over entire dish. Sprinkle Parmesan cheese on top. Bake at 325 for thirty minutes.

SPICY SHRIMP AND PASTA CASSEROLE

(Serves 6)

2 substitutes
1 ½ cups half-and-half
1 cup plain yogurt
½ cup grated Swiss cheese
1/3 cup crumbled feta cheese
1/3 cup chopped fresh parsley leaves
1 teaspoon dried oregano crushed
½ teaspoon garlic powder
9 ounces bow tie pasta cooked
16 ounces mild salsa thick and chunky
2 pounds shrimp cleaned, peeled, and de-veined
½ cup grated Monterey Jack

Spray a 12 by 8-inch pan or glass dish with non-stick cooking spray. Combine the eggs, half-and-half, yogurt, Swiss and feta cheeses, parsley, garlic, basil, and oregano in a large bowl, mixing until thoroughly blended.

Spread 1/2 of the cooked pasta evenly over the bottom of the prepared pan. Cover the pasta with the salsa. Add 1/2 of the shrimp and then cover it with Monterey Jack. Add the remaining pasta and shrimp. Spread the egg mixture over top of the casserole. Bake at 350 degrees for 30 minutes or until bubbly. Let stand for 10 minutes before serving.

ORANGE CHICKEN PASTA

(Serves 6)

3 cups no-pulp orange juice
3 tbsp low sodium soy sauce
2 tbsp dry white wine
2 to 3 tbsp vegetable oil
1 tbsp honey
1 tbsp orange zest; finely grated
1 tbsp gingerroot; peeled and grated
1 ½ lb boneless chicken breasts, skinned
½ lb penne pasta
1 ½ cups frozen peas
2 tbsp fresh Italian parsley, chopped
freshly ground black pepper

In a shallow dish, mix the orange juice, soy sauce, wine, oil, honey, zest, gingerroot, and cayenne. Add the chicken and turn the pieces to coat. Cover and refrigerate 1 to 2 hours, turning the chicken once or twice while marinating.

Remove the chicken from the marinade, reserving the marinade in a small saucepan. Broil or grill the chicken, brushing twice with the marinade, until the inside is no longer pink, about 4 minutes per side; check by cutting into a thick piece. Transfer to a cutting board.

In a large pot of boiling salted water, cook the pasta, uncovered, over high heat, stirring occasionally, until tender but firm, about 8 minutes. Add the peas and heat for a minute or 2. Drain well, rinse with cold water, and transfer to a large bowl.

Cut the chicken into strips. Bring the reserved marinade to a simmer, pour over the pasta mixture, and mix well. Add the chicken strips, parsley, and salt and pepper to taste. Transfer the pasta mixture to a casserole dish sprayed with a non-sick vegetable cooking spray. Cover and bake 30 minutes, or until heated through.

SOUPS

Mary Liz, Tom, Matt, Joan, Anna, Mary, Jerry, Aaron
Andy and Quinn
At Q&A's wedding celebration
December 2007

SOUP STOCKS

Stocks are wonderful things to make up with old bones and meats. Then they may be frozen for later use in recipes calling for them and used as the bases for many tasty sauces.

BASIC BEEF STOCK

8 quarts water
1 beef shank
1 stewing chicken
2 lb. beef bones
2 large carrots
1 large onion, stuck with 3 cloves
1 stalk celery
1 bay leaf
Few parsley stems
Pinch of thyme
5 tbsp. salt

Bring 4 quarts water to a boil and add beef shank, chicken, and bones. Let water return to a boil and boil 5 minutes. Remove from heat and pour water from pot. To the same pot add 4 quarts fresh water and remaining ingredients. Cook slowly 3 hours, uncovered. Strain. Makes a little more than 2 quarts.

BASIC CHICKEN OR TURKEY STOCK

3 lb. chicken or turkey pieces, including bones, wings, necks, and hearts
3 quarts cold water
1 cup celery, coarsely chopped
1 cup carrots, coarsely chopped
2 large onions, stuck with cloves
4 sprigs parsley
1 tablespoon poultry seasoning

Put chicken or turkey pieces into a pot and add the water. Bring to boil and skim. Lower heat, cover, and simmer for 2 hours. Add vegetables and simmer, covered for another hour. Strain and season to taste. Makes about 6 cups. If you have a leftover turkey or chicken carcass, these are great to make soup   stocks   with.

PORK STOCK

2 to 4 quarts uncooked pork bones
2 large carrots, broken in several pieces
2 large onions, unpeeled and halved
2 celery ribs, roughly chopped
2 cloves garlic, unpeeled and smashed
6 peppercorns
2 bay leaves

Heat oven to 450 degrees F. Place bones in single layer in large shallow roasting pan(s); add half of the vegetables and 1 clove of garlic. Roast for 20 to 30 minutes or until bones are well browned. Transfer bones and vegetables to large soup pot; discard any fat.

Pour about 1 cup water into roasting pan(s) and bring to boil over medium-high heat, scraping browned bits free from pan(s). Add to soup pot. Add remaining vegetables, remaining garlic, peppercorns, bay leaves, and enough cold water to cover. Bring to a simmer, occasionally skimming off any foam. Simmer, loosely covered, for 3 to 4 hours, adding more boiling water if liquid evaporates below surface of ingredients.

Strain into large bowl, pouring through large colander; discard solids. Cool slightly; chill for several hours or overnight. Lift off and discard fat.

If not roasting bones, simply place all ingredients in large kettle and proceed with recipe.

To Use a Pressure Cooker: In pressure cooker combine all ingredients (whether roasted or not) with enough water to cover. Pressure-cook for 20 to 30 minutes.

SEAFOOD STOCK

4 to 5 pounds mild white fish (cod or halibut) bones and trimmings, and/or shellfish shells
2 tablespoons butter
2 large onions chopped
4 or 5 chopped garlic cloves
1 stalk celery
1/2 cup chopped parsley
1 teaspoon whole black peppercorns
1 cup dry white wine (optional)
Approximately 1 gallon of water

Melt butter in bottom of stock pot and sauté onion, garlic and celery for about 5 minutes or until soft. Add remaining ingredients and simmer for about an hour. Periodically skim off foam that will appear at the top of pot. Cool and strain out solid ingredients.

VEGETABLE STOCK

1 pound celery
1 1/2 pounds sweet onions
1 pound carrots cut into 1 inch pieces
1 pound tomatoes, cored
½ pound parsnips, cubed
2 tablespoons olive oil
3 cloves garlic
3 whole cloves
2 bay leaves
6 whole black peppercorns
1 bunch fresh parsley, chopped
1 gallon water

Remove leaves and tender inner parts of celery and set aside.

Toss onions, carrots, tomatoes, and turnips with olive oil. Place vegetables in a roasting pan and place them in the 450 degrees oven. Stir the vegetable every 15 minutes. Cook until all of the vegetables have browned and the onions start to caramelize, this will take over one hour.

Put the browned vegetables, celery, garlic, cloves, bay leaf, pepper corns, parsley and water into a large stock pot. Bring to a full boil. Reduce heat to simmer. Cook uncovered until liquid is reduced by half.

Pour the broth through a colander, catching the broth in a large bowl or pot. The liquid caught in the bowl or pot is your vegetable broth it can be used immediately or stored for later use.

Optional Vegetables or Herbs: Garlic cloves, leeks, including the tough green leaves, mushrooms, whole or stems parsley including stems, parsnips, scallions, sweet potatoes, tomatoes (in small amounts only or the stock may be too acidic), winter squash, zucchini or summer squash. Be creative or use what you have on hand.

Note: Vegetables should be rinsed, but there is no need to peel them. Avoid such strongly flavored vegetables as broccoli, cabbage, cauliflower, eggplant, peppers, and turnips.

CREAM OF CHICKEN SOUP

(Serves 4)

4 cups milk
2 tbsp. all-purpose flour
2 tbsp. vegetable oil
2 tbsp. white sugar
2 cups finely chopped, cooked chicken meat
½ tsp. salt
½ tsp. ground black pepper
½ tsp. garlic powder

In a 3 quart saucepan, heat oil. Gradually stir in flour. Let this form a paste, or roux. Then, gradually stir in the milk and continue stirring until thickened.

Add chicken to white sauce mixture. Add sugar, salt, pepper, and garlic powder. Mix well and simmer for 20 minutes over low heat.

If soup is not as thick as desired, mix a small amount of cornstarch with small amount of water and add to soup. Simmer for 10 minutes.

ITALIAN MINESTRONE SOUP

(Serves 8 to 12)

1 cup minced onion
1 cup minced celery
1 cup minced carrot
¼ cup butter or margarine
1 – 48 oz. can tomato juice or V8 juice
6 cups water
½ cup garbanzo beans
½ cup kidney beans
½ cup whole dried peas
½ cup white pea beans
¾ cup sliced carrots
¾ cup chopped onion
¾ cup sliced celery
¾ cup chopped bell pepper
½ cup rice or barley
2 tbsp. minced fresh parsley
1 tsp. dried oregano
1 tsp. dried basil
2 tsp. low sodium soy sauce
Black pepper to taste
1 cup shell macaroni, uncooked
Top with Parmesan cheese

In a large pot, sauté onion, celery, and carrots in butter until browned. Add tomato juice, water, garbanzo beans, kidney beans, dried peas, and white beans. Simmer over low heat for 2 to 2 ½ hours, until everything is tender. Add remaining ingredients, except cheese and pepper; simmer for 40 minutes. Season with pepper, add the macaroni, and simmer for 20 minutes. Ladle into bowls and sprinkle with Parmesan cheese.

ROASTED BUTTERNUT SQUASH SOUP
(Serves 6-8)

1 – 1 ½ butternut squash, peeled seeded and rough chopped
3 tbsp. olive oil
¾ tsp. salt
¼ tsp. freshly ground black pepper
1 cup sweet Italian sausage, removed from the casing
1 cup small diced onion
½ cup small diced carrot
½ cup small diced celery
2 tbsp. minced shallots
1 tbsp. minced garlic
2 tsp. apple cider vinegar
1 ½ quarts low sodium chicken stock
2 tsp. maple syrup
1 tsp. fresh chopped sage leaves

Place the chopped squash in a medium-size mixing bowl. Coat the squash with 2 tablespoons of olive oil and season with pepper. Line a sheet pan with parchment paper and place the squash on top of the sheet pan. Set the sheet pan into the oven and roast for 30 minutes at 425, or until the squash is tender.

Remove the squash from the oven and set aside. Fry the Italian sausage and drain the fat. Add the onions, carrots, and celery in the pan and cook for 5 to 7 minutes. Add the garlic to the pan and cook for 1 minute. Deglaze the pan with the vinegar and add the chicken stock to the pan. Place the squash in the pan along with the maple syrup and sage.

Bring the pan to a boil and reduce to a simmer. Continue to cook the soup for 30 minutes, or until the vegetables are all tender. Taste the soup and re-season if necessary with ½ teaspoon of salt and 1/8 teaspoon pepper. Keep warm until serving.

ROASTED PARSNIP SOUP

(Serves 6-8)

1 lb. parsnip, peeled and roughly chopped
3 tbsp. olive oil
¾ tsp. salt
¼ tsp. freshly cracked white pepper
1 cup diced ham
1 cup onion, diced
½ cup carrots, diced
½ cup celery, diced
1 tbsp. garlic, minced
2 tsp. white vinegar
1 ½ quarts low sodium chicken stock
2 tsp. honey
1 tsp. freshly chopped thyme leaves
½ cup heavy cream

Place the chopped parsnips in a medium-size mixing bowl. Coat the parsnips with 2 tablespoons of olive oil and season with pepper. Line a sheet pan with parchment paper and place the parsnips on top of the sheet pan. Set the sheet pan into the oven and roast for 30 minutes at 425, or until tender.

Remove the parsnips from the oven and set aside. Fry the ham for about 3 minutes. Add the onions, carrots, and celery cook for 5 to 7 minutes. Add the garlic to the pan and cook for 1 minute stirring continuously. Deglaze the pan with the vinegar and add the chicken stock to the pan. Place the parsnips in the pan with the honey and thyme.

Bring the pan to a boil and reduce to a simmer. Continue to cook the soup for 30 minutes, or until the vegetables are all tender. Use an immersion blender to puree the soup to a smooth consistency and velvety texture. Alternately, you can puree the soup in batches using a blender. Taste the soup and re-season if necessary with ½ teaspoon salt and 1/8 teaspoon pepper. Add the cream to the soup and return the soup to a clean saucepan and keep warm until ready to serve.

VEGETABLE AND BEAN SOUP

(Serves 6-8)

2 tbsp. extra-virgin olive oil
1 medium onion, chopped
1 medium potato, peeled and chopped
1 medium zucchini, chopped
1lb chicken cut into small pieces
Salt and pepper
1 – 15 oz. can garbanzo beans (chick peas)
1 – 15 oz. can white beans, cannelloni, drained
6 cups low sodium chicken stock,
1 cup small, then egg noodles for soup, any brand
1 box frozen chopped green beans

Heat medium soup pot over medium-high heat. Add extra-virgin olive oil. Add chicken and pan fry. When chicken is browned add onion, potato and zucchini and season with salt and pepper. Cook 5 or 6 minutes alone, stirring frequently, then add the canned beans and the chicken stock. Cover the pot and bring the soup up to a boil.

When the soup is at a boil, remove the lid. Stir in the noodles and green beans and reduce heat to low. Simmer soup an additional 5 to 6 minutes then remove it from the heat.

SQUASH SOUP

(Serves 6)

1 medium onion, finely chopped
¼ cup butter or margarine
2 tbsp. all-purpose flour
Dash of pepper
¼ tsp. ground nutmeg
2 cups low sodium chicken stock
1 cup milk
1 ½ cups cooked, cubed yellow squash
1 ½ cups cooked, cubed zucchini
2 tsp. Worcestershire sauce
1 egg yolk, slightly beaten
½ cup light or heavy cream

Sauté the onion in butter until soft, about 5 minutes in Dutch oven. Add the flour, pepper, and nutmeg. Stir until blended and bubbly. Remove from heat and gradually stir in the chicken stock and milk. Return to heat, bringing to a boil and cook, stirring until thickened. Add the squash, zucchini and Worcestershire sauce. Reduce heat to low and cook, stirring often until heated through. Blend together the egg yolk and cream. Stir in some of the hot soup into the egg mixture, and then stir the mixture back into the hot soup. Cook until soup is heated through and egg hat thickened. May be served as a cold soup.

AUTUMN PUMPKIN SOUP

(Serves 6-8)

1 onion chopped
3 cups sliced fresh mushrooms
1 stick butter
½ cup flour
2 quarts low sodium chicken broth
1 can pumpkin
1 ½ teaspoons curry powder
Pepper to taste
½ cup half and half
2 tablespoons honey
Sour cream

Sauté the onions and mushrooms in ½ stick butter until the onions are tender and translucent. Transfer onion/mushroom mix to a bow. Using the same pan melt the rest of the butter and add flour to make a paste. Whisk the chicken broth slowly into the flour mixture. Cook until thickened while stirring constantly. Add the onion/mushroom mixture, pumpkin, curry and pepper. Stir. Add the half and half along with the honey. Cook until heated. Top with a dollop of sour cream. Serve with hot French bread.

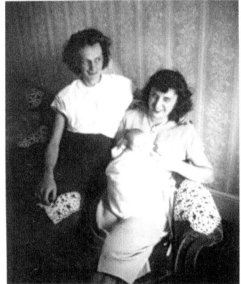

Aunt Helen (Dad's Sister), Ellie holding Donna Kay

TUSCAN SAUSAGE AND POTATO SOUP

(Serves 6)

4 to 5 cups low sodium chicken stock
2 cups potatoes, diced
1 cup chopped spinach or other greens
1 lb. Italian sausage (sweet or hot)
Fresh Italian parsley, chopped
½ cup heavy cream (or half-and-half mixed with a tbsp. of flour or skim milk mixed with 2 tbsp. of flour)
¼ tsp. garlic powder

Remove the sausage from its casing and sauté the sausage in a skillet or Dutch oven and brown. Drain on paper towels. Add to a large stock pot the chicken broth, sausage, potatoes, and parsley. Simmer soup until potatoes are tender at least 30 minutes. Add spinach and cook until completely wilted. Add cream or half-and-half and simmer a few minutes until thickened.

SPLIT PEA SOUP

(Serves 10 to 12)

½ gallon water
1 ham hock or bone from leftover ham
1 lb. dry split peas
1 cup chopped onion
1 carrot, chopped
1 garlic clove
1 tsp salt
¼ tsp. thyme
1 bay leaf
1 tsp. sugar
¼ tsp. marjoram
¼ tsp fresh pepper
Lemon juice to taste
Worcestershire sauce to taste
Milk as desired

Put all ingredients except milk in large pot, and simmer 3 hours partially covered. Stir occasionally. Remove bay leaf and ham bone. Cut meat off bone and return to soup. Add milk to then to desired consistency for serving. Add additional cubed ham if desired.

ITALIAN COUNTRY SOUP

(Serves 6)

8 cups low sodium chicken broth
4 sausage links, precooked and sliced thinly
1 lb. Chicken cut into pieces
1 cup chopped celery
1 cup chopped carrots
1 cup green beans cut into pieces
¼ cup thinly sliced leeks
1 medium zucchini, diced
2 small yellow squash, diced
1 can cannelloni beans
2 tomatoes, chopped
1 cup pasta
3 cups shredded greens (mustard green, spinach or chard)
Pepper
Fresh grated Parmesan cheese

Add the vegetables except the canned beans and greens to the broth, and cook 20 minutes. Add the canned beans, pasta, sausages, chicken, and greens and cook another 15 minutes. Season with salt and pepper. Serve warm topped fresh grated cheese.

OSSO BUCO SOUP

(Serves 4)

Pork Meatballs

1 lb ground pork
1 large egg, beaten
1/3 cup Italian bread crumbs,
¼ cup, grated Parmesan
¼ to ½ tsp. freshly grated nutmeg,
Black pepper

Soup
2 tbsp. extra-virgin olive oil,
2 carrots, diced
2 ribs celery diced and their greens
1 medium yellow onion, chopped
Pepper
1 bay leaf
½ cup white wine
1 – 14 oz. can white beans, drained
1 – 15 oz. can low sodium diced tomatoes
3 cups low sodium chicken stock,
2 cups low sodium beef stock,
1 cup egg noodles

Combine the veal and the next 5 ingredients make into meat balls and pan fry. Remove meat balls from pan and add carrots, celery, and onion. Season with pepper and add bay leaf. Add beans, tomatoes and the wine, chicken and beef stock to the pot. Add meatballs to the pot along with the noodles. Cook until the noodles are done (about 6 minutes).

MINESTRONE SOUP

(Serves 6)

2 quarts low sodium beef broth
½ cup ham, chopped
1 cup celery (use leaves also), chopped
½ cup fresh kidney beans
¾ cup fresh peas

Combine and simmer the above ingredients for 45 minutes.

1 cup spinach, chopped
1 small zucchini squash, chopped
¼ cup fresh onion, minced
1 carrot, diced
1 cup cabbage (green or red), chopped
1 cup tomatoes, diced (use low sodium if using canned)
1 tbsp. olive oil

Sauté the above vegetables in the olive oil. Then add the vegetables to the hot stock.

Add:
¼ cup dry rice or pasta
1 tbsp. fresh parsley, chopped, or 1 tsp. dried parsley
1 tbsp. fresh sage, minced, or 1 tsp. dried sage

Add the rice or pasta, parsley, and sage to the soup cook for 56 minutes. Sprinkle with grated Parmesan cheese before serving.

Printed in Great Britain
by Amazon

23518572R00079